UNDER LINCOLN'S HAT

Also by the Abraham Lincoln Presidential Library Foundation and Carla Knorowski:
Gettysburg Replies: The World Responds to Abraham Lincoln's Gettysburg Address

Also by James M. Cornelius:
Undying Words: Lincoln 1858–1865, co-authored with Olivia Mahoney
Abraham Lincoln Presidential Library and Museum: Official Commemorative Guide,
in collaboration with Thomas F. Schwartz

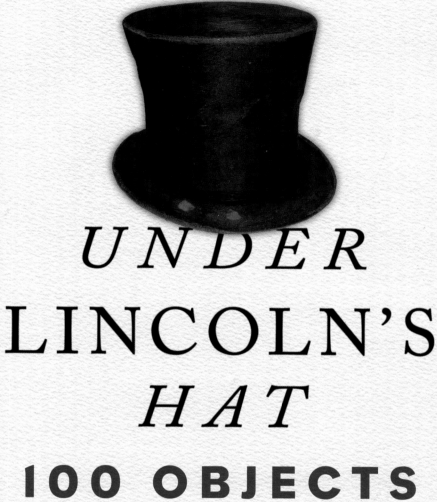

UNDER LINCOLN'S *HAT*

100 OBJECTS

THAT TELL THE STORY OF HIS LIFE AND LEGACY

JAMES M. CORNELIUS and **CARLA KNOROWSKI**

Abraham Lincoln Presidential Library Foundation

Guilford, Connecticut

An imprint of Rowman & Littlefield

Distributed by NATIONAL BOOK NETWORK

Copyright © 2016 by Abraham Lincoln Presidential Library Foundation

British Library Cataloguing in Publication Information Available
Library of Congress Cataloging-in-Publication Data

ISBN 978-1-4930-2466-7 (hardcover)
ISBN 978-1-4930-2780-4 (e-book)

♾™ The paper used in this publication meets the minimum requirements of American National Standard for Information Sciences—Permanence of Paper for Printed Library Materials, ANSI/NISO Z39.48-1992.

Contents

PART 8: ICON

Preface   BY LOUISE TAPER, LINCOLN COLLECTOR

As a Lincoln collector, from the very first I had admired the State of Illinois and their Lincoln collection. To me it was home for all things Lincoln. When the Abraham Lincoln Presidential Library and Museum was built, it became the ideal place to house their magnificent holdings.

For years people asked me what I intended to do with my Lincoln collection. While many collections had been put up for auction and then scattered, the Abraham Lincoln Presidential Library and Museum is now the perfect place for collections to remain together. Now, proudly, a large part of my collection resides there.

You can come there to see all phases of Lincoln's life, from his earliest manuscript—the Cypher Book Page—through the assassination, and including items from all his ancestors and descendants. You learn about Lincoln the young boy, the lawyer, the husband, the father, and the president.

Museums need curators and curators need collectors. We travel this road together, hand in hand, offering the public what they would never experience otherwise.

Lincoln's memory is kept alive through the gathering and assembling of manuscripts, artifacts, rare books, paintings, and sculpture. These extraordinary pieces of Lincolniana touch our hearts.

It has been a joy and a privilege for me to collect Lincoln and be a part of his story. But, it is an even greater joy knowing that the Abraham Lincoln Presidential Library and Museum will be sharing its treasures with generations to come. ∽

Introduction   BY JAMES M. CORNELIUS, PhD

HOW DO WE KNOW WHAT A PERSON FROM THE PAST WAS REALLY LIKE? We might learn as much about a woman, for example, by examining the pattern on the china she chose as by reading one of her letters. Both reveal her mind, for in its way the china set is a letter written on the dollars she handed over to acquire it. Neither letter nor decoration tells the whole story, but they are not mutually exclusive, either. Her handwriting might even mimic some feature of the egg-and-dart or the color-and-base artistry on her teacup.

This might not work as well for someone like Abraham Lincoln, who wrote vastly more letters than he acquired stuff. The only exception might be the newspaper words he ingested, or the sermons, prayers, and poems he ingested, which became the feed-stock for his own words. We cannot recapture the physical and formative incidents of Lincoln's life, but we can place one of his many letters next to a personal possession as a way to throw two-lensed light on the man and his era.

This volume therefore is an effort to provide one hundred "keys" to Lincoln that will jimmy the lock to the mystery of his mind, even if we cannot quite open that mind to full light and questioning. We can look closely at Lincoln's clock placed next to a legal document he wrote within its soundscape to see what this combination reveals. We can only imagine what kinds of paper-and-ink documents his battered briefcase held during his lifelong fight against slavery. We can touch objects that give proof of his love for his wife and children. We can flip through some of the books he owned, both serious and light, that sit next to his 272-word Gettysburg Address, which is as big as a library in its own right. If the axiom "the clothes make the man" has any currency in Lincoln's case, his battered hat still sits atop his brilliant head in our imag-inations, and it ought always be considered symbolically and literally as an element of his thought when reading his directives about a war for Union and Freedom. It is our hope that every reader will see patterns and connections from each page in this volume and perhaps view the man in new or more in-depth ways.

And if his hat does not tell you all that you wish to know about, say, his views on colonization or the best campaigning or military strategies, well then, neither did the man's entire corpus of writings. He simply kept some things . . . well . . . under his hat.

Our hunger for knowing more about Lincoln far outstrips the short time he had to leave us a full record for posterity.

We turn instead to what does remain and use our powers of inference while trying not to do his great mind an injustice. "I was born Feb. 12, 1809," he wrote in 1860. The story got more interesting and complicated from there. ⌒

Introduction   BY CARLA KNOROWSKI, PHD

LEFT AT THE END OF ANY ONE PERSON'S LIFE ARE HIS OR HER SO-CALLED "personal effects." For most people, they are gathered up, distributed among loved ones, discarded or given away to charity. Over the years, most are lost to time. A few priceless items may remain, passed down from generation to generation, but for the most part, they are scattered to the winds. That is, unless you are Abraham Lincoln.

Thousands upon thousands of Lincoln's personal effects—from the slate on which he wrote as a youngster to the axe he used to chop wood for soldiers shortly before he died—have been gathered over time and safeguarded as his renown grew, and most certainly after that fateful moment when he suddenly and so tragically "belonged to the ages." The stories these documents and artifacts tell help to crystallize Lincoln as both an ordinary man and an iconic martyr. They form an ever clearer picture of the deeply complex yet extraordinarily simple and down-to-earth man who, from a very young age, understood, or at least hoped, that he was destined for greatness.

With more than fifty-two thousand artifacts and documents stored in the collections of the Abraham Lincoln Presidential Library and Museum (ALPLM), it was a challenge to select only one hundred items to tell the story of Lincoln and unlock the mystery of the man. But we have done our best.

In the course of writing this book, we found ourselves reworking the list, constantly adding in objects and taking some out. In the end, we selected those artifacts and documents which told his story not only in a practical light, but in a symbolic one. We also selected lesser-known artifacts and documents which we felt might reveal even in an isolated manner, a single thread of the man as an inextricable part of the greater fabric of his being: his favorite poem, patent drawing, and a record of his legal work. Conversely we selected iconic items such as the Gettysburg Address, Emancipation Proclamation, and Thirteenth Amendment that set the foundation upon which his immortality was built.

We have really only scratched the surface, but believe we have made a good start. We invite you now to turn the page and begin to explore *Under Lincoln's Hat*. We hope this journey inspires you to then take a step further and visit the Abraham Lincoln Presidential Library and Museum in Springfield, Illinois, right in the heart of the Land of Lincoln. Mr. Lincoln is beckoning. What are you waiting for? ⌒

About the Abraham Lincoln Presidential Library Foundation and the Abraham Lincoln Presidential Library and Museum

THE ABRAHAM LINCOLN PRESIDENTIAL LIBRARY FOUNDATION supports the educational and cultural programming of the Abraham Lincoln Presidential Library and Museum; fosters Lincoln scholarship through the acquisition and publication of documentary materials related to Lincoln and his era; and promotes a greater appreciation of history through exhibits, conferences, publications, online services, and other activities designed to promote historical literacy. The Abraham Lincoln Presidential Library houses the largest collection of Abraham and Mary Lincoln manuscripts in the world. This world-class collection of artifacts, photographs, books, commemorative items, and related manuscript materials attracts authors, researchers, and students who are looking for new information on every facet of the sixteenth president's life and times.

The Abraham Lincoln Presidential Museum is located in the historic downtown district of Springfield, Illinois, within walking distance of the Old State Capitol, the Lincoln-Herndon Law Office, the Lincoln Home National Park Site, and the Illinois State Capitol. Over four million guests have visited this ground-breaking museum since its opening. The museum has captured the attention of its audience with more than 40,000 square feet of immersive exhibits, thousands of original manuscripts and possessions of the Lincolns, engaging theatrical presentations, educational programs, and lectures. ∽

Robert

Mary

Willie

Tad

PART 1
❧ FAMILY MAN ❧

A. Lincoln

PRESIDENT LINCOLN'S DOG.

Fido

Fanning the Flame

Mr. Hazel's Student

1816

As is well documented, Abraham Lincoln was largely self-taught, having received only about a year of formal schooling over the course of his lifetime. There are many reasons for this, chief among them that the Lincoln family was poor. Thomas and Nancy Lincoln did not have much in the way of discretionary funds to pay their children's teachers. Also, they needed young Abraham to help work the family farm. Education was not yet a universal mandate in early-nineteenth-century America. Lincoln much preferred going to school or carrying out his own studies to working on the farm. He was more devoted to intellectual pursuits than physical labor, but as a dutiful son he served the family first before concentrating on his studies.

Some of the earliest formal instruction Lincoln received occurred in his birth state of Kentucky. He attended what were then loosely called "ABC" schools where he was taught by at least two men, the first being Zachariah Riney, and the second Caleb Hazel, as attested by Lincoln himself for the newsman John Locke Scripps in 1860.

In 1816 after the fall harvest, Abraham, the boy-who-would-be-president, age seven, and his sister, Sarah, age nine, received instruction from Hazel, using a small slate measuring twelve inches by fifteen and a half inches by a half inch. The slate has a traditional black writing surface and is framed in oak. A circular hole is punched through the top of the frame so the slate could hang vertically from a nail in the classroom for easy viewing. It was probably manufactured around 1810 near Slatington, Pennsylvania, where slate is mined even to this day. The slate would be used by both teacher and students alike and in this regard is probably the surface on which some of Abraham Lincoln's earliest public writings were ever written, but alas, erased.

It is easy to imagine Mr. Hazel filling the slate with words and numbers, fanning the flame of young Abraham's insatiable curiosity and instilling in him a love for learning and an understanding of the value of education that more than a half-century later resulted in President Lincoln's signing into law the Morrill Land Grant Act in 1862. The Act established at least one public land grant university in every state, thereby making a higher education available to the masses. The slate was a treasured keepsake of the Hazel family for two centuries, being passed down through six generations of family members. ∽

"... used by both teacher and students alike ... is probably the surface on which some of Abraham Lincoln's earliest public writings were ever written but alas, erased."

2

Father and Son

Craftsman in Wood, Craftsman in Word

1820

As the year 1816 came to a close, Thomas and Nancy Lincoln moved from their home state of Kentucky and settled with their children, Sarah and Abraham, along Pigeon Creek, in Spencer County, Indiana. Although their years in Indiana began with much hope and promise, they were in the end difficult for the family. During that time, Abraham grew from a young boy to a self-sustaining, twenty-one-year-old. His birth mother Nancy contracted milk sickness and died. His father remarried, and not only did Abraham suddenly have a new mother, he had three new step-siblings. All the while, his father Thomas struggled financially. While mostly known as a dirt farmer by profession, Thomas Lincoln was also a skilled carpenter, who supported the family in part through his craftsmanship.

Two pieces designed and built by Abraham's father during the Indiana years are a plantation desk and a day bed made of cherry wood. Thomas made the desk when Abraham was just eleven years old. No doubt young Abraham watched his father build it; perhaps he even helped. While appreciating his father's woodworking skills and the means to an end in the worthy profession, Abraham was much more taken with intellectual pursuits. It is likely that Thomas Lincoln built furniture for his own homestead, with his son perhaps learning to write on a handmade desk or table. The Thomas Lincoln desk incorporates an enclosed double-door glass-panel bookcase attached to the base of the desk, which includes a tilted writing surface that can be flipped up for storage. The desk stands at a little more than six feet in height, slightly shorter than the eventual height of Thomas's son, Abraham. The day bed is in the Classical Revival style, standing approximately twenty-nine inches in height with a length of eighty-three inches.

Although Abraham was much more the thinking man who preferred pen and paper, he could wield an axe extraordinarily well and had woodworking skills competent enough to handcraft a wooden prototype for his 1849 patent. He also assisted his father in building the pulpit for Pigeon Creek Baptist Church. Still, Abraham's father was the true craftsman of the family. The two pieces of furniture in the Abraham Lincoln Presidential Library and Museum's (ALPLM) collection are rare artifacts skillfully handcrafted by Thomas Lincoln, and they evoke thoughts of a father-son relationship which at best could be described as respectful, yet distant. ∞

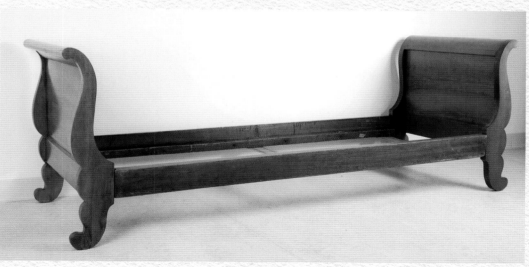

Cherrywood plantation desk and daybed crafted by Abraham Lincoln's father, Thomas, during the family's Indiana years

3

"For Fools to Read"

A Page from Lincoln's Cypher Book

1824–1826

THE OLDEST KNOWN PIECE OF ABRAHAM LINCOLN'S WRITING IN EXIStence today is found on the pages in a handmade "sum book," better known as a "cypher book." These pages, circa 1824–1826, were sewn together and used by a teenage Lincoln while he lived in southern Indiana. He used the book to practice mathematical calculations. His stepmother Sarah Bush Johnston Lincoln, like any proud and sentimental mother would, kept the book as a keepsake until after her son's death, before giving it to his longtime friend and Springfield law partner William H. Herndon.

There is no telling the length of the original book, but there are known to be eleven remaining leaves in existence. Scholars have determined that the page shown here is the fourth page in a book of calculations scrawled in ink by the young Lincoln. On one side of this particular cypher book page, the young schoolboy writes, "Abraham Lincoln's Book," a statement of ownership all too often denied him because his family was too poor to afford books or even paper. What is most interesting perhaps is the following rhyme composed by the future sixteenth president:

> Abraham Lincoln is my nam[e]
> And with my pen I wrote the same
> I wrote in both hast[e] and speed
> And left it here for fools to read.

These lines provide a glimpse into Lincoln, who, even at an early age had a growing sense of humor and sense of self. He no doubt wrote these verses with a smile and a wink, perhaps aware that a teacher, authority figure, or some other "fool" would be reviewing and reading his work and the joke would be on them. Perhaps on some level, this teenage Lincoln was hopeful that people in the future would be reading what he wrote, however important or in this case, inane. ⌘

Divide By 4423) 89779 (x) 20254

20254
4433

Abraham Lincoln is my
nam
And with my pen I wrote
the same
I wrote on both hast and
and left it here for fools
to read   1824

4 A Solid Dock, A Boat Adrift

The Step-Family, Part I

JANUARY 12, 1851

AFTER LINCOLN'S MOTHER NANCY DIED IN 1818, HIS FATHER THOMAS remarried. Sarah Bush Johnston was a Kentuckian he had known much of his life, recently widowed and with three children slightly older than Abraham and his sister. Sarah's alcoholic husband had left her with debts, which Thomas paid off before they loaded her few things on to a wagon and headed for Indiana.

Abraham's stepbrother, John D., was two years younger, and, as Abraham put it charitably, "an idler." John D. may have been the force that caused some of the friction between Abraham and his father.

In the letter shown here, Lincoln wrote to his "Dear Brother" that he could not come see his ill father because he had a sick wife and newborn at home, and that they had lost baby Eddy about a year prior. At the age of seventy-three, Thomas Lincoln died two or three days after his son's letter arrived.

Abraham had purchased some land from his father, prior to his death, at four times the market price and saw to it that a rental income would always go to Thomas and Sarah. This income now supported Sarah. Abraham also sold John D. eighty acres for one dollar to keep him afloat financially. John D. sold it within a year and spent the proceeds.

Though we do not have all of the family correspondence, what shards we have incontrovertibly tell a sorry tale of a rural American couple in declining years, pulled between one son, a solid dock, and another son, a boat adrift. John D. died at age forty-three, leaving a wife, eight children, and an estate worth fifty-six dollars. ∝

"Abraham's stepbrother, John D., was two years younger, and, as Abraham put it charitably, 'an idler.'"

---

man who puts his trust in Him— Say to him that
if we could meet now, it is doubtful whether it would
not be more painful than pleasant; but that if it
be his lot to go now, he will soon have a joyous
[meeting] with many loved ones gone before; and where
[the rest] of us, through the help of God, hope ere long
[to join] them—

Write me again when you receive this—

Affectionately,

A. Lincoln

Springfield, Jan 7. 12. 1851

Dear Brother:

On the day before yesterday I received
a letter from Harriett, written at Greenup— She says she
has just returned from your house, and that Father
low, and will hardly recover— She also says
you have written me two letters; and that
you do not expect me to come now, [you]
that I do not write— I received both your
although I have not answered them, it is no
I have forgotten them, or been uninterested about them—
but because it appeared to me I could write nothing whole could do any good— You already know
I desire that neither Father or Mother shall [be in want]
of any comfort either in health or sickness while they
live; and I feel sure you have not failed to use my
name, if necessary, to procure a doctor or any thing else
for Father in his present sickness— My business is
such that I could hardly leave home now, if it were
[not], as it is, that my own wife is sick abed— (It
is a case of baby-sickness, and I suppose is not dangerous—) I sincerely hope Father may yet recover his health;
but at all events tell him to remember to call
upon, and confide in, our great, and good, and merciful
Maker; who will not turn away from him in any
[ex]tremity— He notes the fall of a sparrow, and numbers the
hairs of our heads; and he will not forget the dying

Shelbyville, Nov. 4. 1851.

Dear Brother:

When I came into Charleston day before yesterday I learned that you are anxious to sell the land where you live and move to Missouri— I have been thinking of this ever since, and can not but think such a notion is utterly foolish— What can you do in Missouri better than here? Is the land any richer? Can you there, any more than here, raise corn & wheat & oats, without work? Will any body there, any more than here, do your work for you? If you intend to go to work, there is no better place than right where you are; if you do not intend to go to work, you can not get along any where— Squirming & crawling about from place to place can do no good— You have raised no crop this year, and what you really want is to sell the land, get the money and spend it— part with the land you have, and my life upon it, you will never after own a spot big enough to bury you in— Half you will get for the land, you spend in moving to Missouri, and the other half you will eat and drink and wear out, & no foot of land will be bought. Now I feel it is my duty to have no hand in such a piece of foolery— I feel that it is so even on your own account, and particularly on Mother's account. The Eastern forty acres, I intend to keep for Mother while she lives— if you will not cultivate it, it will rent for enough to support her at least it will rent for something— Her Dower in the other two forties, she can let you have, and no thanks to

me— Now do not misunderstand this letter— I do not write it in any unkindness— I write it in order if possible to get you to face the truth— which truth is, you are destitute because you have idled away all your time— Your thousand pretences for not getting along better, are all nonsense— they deceive nobody but yourself— Go to work is the only cure for your case—

A word for Mother:

Chapman tells me he wants you to go and live with him— If I were you I would try it awhile. If you get tired of it (as I think you will not) you can return to your own home— Chapman feels very kindly to you, and I have no doubt he will make your situation very pleasant—

Sincerely your Son
A. Lincoln

Equal under God's Eyes

The Step-Family, Part II

November 4, 1851

5

RETURNING TO THE AREA ON LEGAL BUSINESS, LINCOLN VISITED HIS step-family after which he wrote to John D., "I learned that you are anxious to sell the land where you live, and move to Missouri; I . . . can not but think that such a notion is utterly foolish." John D. soon moved to Arkansas but came back to live off of his mother within a year. Lincoln admonishes his stepbrother, "*Go to work* is the only cure for your case." Yet John D. would neither find a job nor stop spending money.

Lincoln then asks to relay "A word for Mother," who could not read, in which he reports that her granddaughter and husband have offered to take her in at their home in Charleston. Sarah did go to live with relatives nearby for some years, but she eventually returned to the cabin where she and her husband Thomas had lived. She died there in 1869.

What are we to make of the Johnstons? Sarah, unable to read or write, had a loving heart for all around her. Her son John D., literate and strong, shunned work and caused want for all around him. His two sisters, Elizabeth and Matilda, had clear enough memories of Abraham in later years, and some of their many descendants are to this day assets to the rural county of their roots. But for the somewhat chance marriage of a descendant of German immigrants to Thomas Lincoln, all of them would be forgotten. Yet in a family record mostly filled in for them by the future president in 1851, the names appear equal under God's eyes. That is surely how Sarah saw the lines on the paper. ∞

"Go to work is the only cure for your case."

---

6 The "Fatal First"

Letters to a Confidant

MARCH 27, 1842

JOSHUA SPEED WAS LINCOLN'S CLOSEST FRIEND. THEY MET LARGELY BY chance, as young Kentuckians who both migrated to Springfield, Illinois, around 1837, and parted as boon companions, flat-mates, and consultants on love, law, politics, and life in 1841. Their sectional divide—one returned to a successful plantation in Kentucky, the other rose to president of the United States—did some harm but no permanent damage to their friendship.

Here Lincoln explains an ecliptic moment in his life: "that fatal first of Jan'y '41." We think this means simply the date that his nuptials to Mary Todd were called off. Speed liked Mary, but he was very much aware of Lincoln's chief political and professional concern that day, too: the impending bankruptcy of the State of Illinois. As the Whig leader in the lower house of the legislature, Lincoln led the minority in full-bore support of tax-supported improvements such as roads, canals, and rail lines that proved to be more than the young state could afford. Illinois was hardly alone in this. Maryland and Mississippi, for example, had repudiated their debts in the same era. Lincoln, the economic spokesman of his party, a prime mover of this push for modernization, knew that he bore some blame.

Meanwhile, Mary Todd was distraught over the cancelled nuptials, a condition that ate away at Abraham's heart. At the time of this letter, Speed had just married in Kentucky, and Lincoln praised his friend's course and wished him all happiness. And, then, about nine months later, Abraham walked down the aisle with Mary, thanks to various friends' help.

There are seventeen letters from Lincoln to Speed. Of the return correspondence we have only one second-hand example, since Abraham and Mary burned their incoming mail in 1861. The Speed letters, revealed in the early twentieth century, form the truest portrait of Lincoln as a thinker-in-ink, as a swain, as an attorney for a friend, and as one of a circle of bright young fellows who saw the nation's brightness ahead of them, although only one of them would survive the darkest patch, the Civil War. ∞

Springfield, March 27th 1842

Dear Speed:

Yours of the 10th Inst. was received
three or four days since. You know I am sincere,
when I tell you, the pleasure its contents gave me
was and is inexpressible— As to your farm matter,
I have no sympathy with you— I have no farm,
nor ever expect to have; and consequently have
not studied the subject enough to be much interested with it— I can only say that I am glad
you are satisfied and pleased with it—

But on that other subject, to me of the most
intense interest, whether in joy or sorrow, I never
had the power to withhold my sympathy from
you— It can not be told, how it now thrills me
with joy, to hear you say you are "far happier
than you ever expected to be." That much I know is
enough. I know you too well to suppose your expecta-
tions were not, at least sometimes, extravagant,
and if the reality exceeds them all I say enough
dear Lord— I am not going beyond the truth, when
I tell you, that the short space it took me
to read my your last letter, gave me more pleasure than the total sum of all I have enjoyed
since that fatal first of Jan'y '41. Since then,
it seems to me, I should have been entirely happy,
but for the never-absent idea, that there is one

7

The Bond of Holy Matrimony

A Little Slip of Paper

NOVEMBER 4, 1842

THIS SIMPLE DOCUMENT IN THE HANDS OF THE COURT CLERK AND THE minister sealed the fates of Abraham and Mary Todd Lincoln. Much has been written—perhaps too much—about their earlier romantic interests, even with each other. Much more has been written about their life together. This piece of paper, in its way, has launched a million pages. The Lincolns as a couple continue to fascinate us because of their surface differences:

He was 6'4", she was 5'4".

He was born in a log cabin with a dirt floor; she in a fine home with many black servants.

She was socially ambitious; he, politically so.

They were also similar: He loved her; she loved him.

It was common to hold a wedding in a private home in that day. In this case the home was a manse that belonged to Mary's sister Elizabeth and her husband, Ninian W. Edwards. The Reverend Charles Dresser who presided over the ceremony barely had an Episcopal church in which to hold Sunday services, so he was accustomed to this type of thing. Dresser's brother Henry built him a cottage at 8th and Jackson. About fourteen months after this particular nuptial, he sold it to the young Lincolns. Dresser was out of town visiting family in the East when the Lincolns' second son, Eddy, died in February 1850. And so the grieving parents turned to the new Presbyterian minister in town, Reverend James Smith, for solace and a home funeral, and thereafter became more regularly religious in his rather grander church.

Of such torrid emotional events does a little slip of paper whisper. ∽

THE PEOPLE OF THE STATE OF ILLINOIS.

To any Minister of the Gospel, or other authorised Person---GREETING.

THESE are to License and permit you to join in the holy bands of Matrimony *Abraham Lincoln* and *Mary Todd* of the County of Sangamon and State of Illinois, and for so doing, this shall be your sufficient warrant.

Given under my hand and seal of office, at Springfield, in said County this 4th day of *November* 1842

N. W. Matheny Clerk.

Solemnized on the same 4th day of Nov. 1842 *Charles Dresser*

8

Spoons over Time

The Fleeting Nature of Life

1842–1865

FUNCTIONALITY ASIDE, EVERYDAY ITEMS CAN CARRY QUITE A STORIED history owing in part to when and by whom they were used. This is certainly the case with the variety of spoons used by the Lincolns and their extended family over the course of their lives. The ALPLM's collection abounds with spoons, all historically valuable simply because they are Lincoln family heirlooms. One set of note is the five Platt & Brothers coin silver soup spoons owned by Mary's sister Elizabeth Edwards. Edwards had hosted the marriage ceremony of Mary Todd and Abraham Lincoln in her home in Springfield, Illinois, on November 4, 1842. The fiddle back handle soup spoons, engraved with the surname "Edwards," were most likely used as part of the celebratory meal enjoyed by the Edwardses and Lincolns on the occasion of Abraham and Mary's nuptials.

Also part of the collection is a set of ten bouillon soup spoons produced by the Gorham Manufacturing Co. and once owned by Mary Lincoln. Her initials "ML" are engraved on the handles. These spoons reveal the decorative tastes of their owners and speak to the history of a family. But none of these spoons match the poignancy and power of one lone spoon in the collection—the last spoon Abraham Lincoln used in his life as attested to by Mary Lincoln's friend and confidante Elizabeth Keckly on April 16, 1865, just one day after the president died at the hand of an assassin. In a clear, strong, right-slanted cursive, Keckly wrote these somber and sobering words:

"The last spoon used by Abraham Lincoln at his noon lunch at the White House the day he was killed."

This spoon is an example of how an everyday implement usually of little or no importance can become larger than life and of historic proportions. A spoon is only a spoon until it is the last one Abraham Lincoln held in his strong and ample hand. What might he have done on April 14, 1865, had he known it was to be the last to touch his fingertips or pass his lips? Elizabeth Keckly's gesture of saving the spoon for our nation's posterity showed the depth of her compassion, her understanding of symbolism and history, and her knowledge that perhaps the least consequential things in life can be and are the most profound particularly when they turn on the click of an assassin's gun. ⌘

Mary Lincoln's friend and confidante Elizabeth Keckly

The last spoon used by Abraham Lincoln at his noon lunch at the White House the day he was killed April 16th "65."

Elizabeth Keckley

9

A. LINCOLN

Immortal Name, Immortal Man

1844

THE DOOR PLATE FROM THE SPRINGFIELD, ILLINOIS, HOME OF ABRAham and Mary Lincoln alerted visitors to the Greek Revival house at 8th and Jackson Streets that they were entering the home of "Honest Abe," "The Railsplitter." While Abraham Lincoln had many titles, he had but one name. That name still carries as much weight today as it did more than 170 years ago when Abraham and Mary first purchased the home for a sum of fifteen hundred dollars from the Reverend Charles Dresser and affixed the nameplate on its front door. The rectangular plate is not very large at 2.75 by 6.375 inches. It was not necessarily readable from the wooden boardwalk out front but most certainly was as you climbed the stairs to the entrance. The Lincolns' Springfield house was the first and only home owned by Abraham and Mary, where they lived for some seventeen years up until they and their sons left for Washington, DC, soon to be inaugurated as the "First Family." The city of Springfield, just four years prior to the Lincolns' purchase of their home, had a population of 2,579. The custom of numbering houses had not yet come into practice, so the simplicity of using a first initial and last name was sufficient to tell visitors to whom the house belonged. It also mirrored the manner in which Abraham Lincoln most often signed his name: "A. LINCOLN"—an immortal name for an immortal man. ∞

M. DUBOCE, Photographer,
SPRINGFIELD, - - - ILLINOIS.

Washington, April 16- 1848-

Dear Mary:

In this troublesome world, we are never quite satisfied— When you were here, I thought you hindered me some in attending to business; but now, having nothing but business— no variety— it has grown exceedingly tasteless to me— I hate to sit down and direct documents, and I hate to stay in this old room by myself— You know I told you in last sunday's letter, I was going to make a little speech during the week; but the week has passed away without my getting a chance to do so; and now, my interest in the subject has passed away too— Your second and third letters have been received since I wrote before. Dear Eddy thinks, father is "gone tapila" Has any further discovery been made as to the breaking into your grand-mother's house? If I were she, I would not remain there alone— You mention that your uncle John Parker is likely to be at Lexington— Don't forget to present him my very kindest regards—

I went yesterday to hunt the little plaid stockings, as you wished; but found that McKnight has quit business, and Allen had not a single pair of the description you give, and only one plain pair of any sort that I thought would fit "Eddy's dear little feet." I have a notion to

"Dear Mary"

Abraham Writes to His Wife

APRIL 16, 1848

THE LINCOLNS, LIKE MOST PEOPLE, VALUED THEIR PRIVACY. PERHAPS they had deeper reasons to protect their personal lives when they moved to Washington, DC, in February 1861. For when they did move, they burned their personal correspondence, and apparently some lower-level political correspondence too.

Yet a few rare items were saved from the "burn-pile," as Mr. Lincoln is reported to have called it when offering a neighbor the chance to go out and pick a souvenir if he could find one. Another story has it that when the Lincolns moved out temporarily in 1847 to take up a seat in Congress, they inadvertently left some papers on the top shelf of a closet . . . but this pair of letters (see second letter on page 23) from 1848 could not be in that category.

In short, what we have here is a sample of the most personal, unmediated communication between them. No other pre-presidential letter from Abraham to Mary is known to survive. Only two others from him to her survive. The other dozen or so, though interesting, date from the White House years and are, in the main, laconically short, composed, and were sent as telegrams through the US Military and thus seen and read by the sending clerk, the receiving clerk, and possibly other passersby.

In 1848 on another occasion he saluted her as "My Dear Wife," but here it is "Dear Mary." Evidence shows us that more letters passed through the mail too, with money changing hands. We learn at least from these that their second son's name should be spelled "Eddy" rather than "Eddie" as was long thought; that the oldest was "Bobby" rather than "Bobbie" or "Boby." Worryingly, Abraham sees that Mary is "being so openly intimate with the Wickliffe family," which he regarded as her father's worst political, personal, and legal antagonists. ⌘

"My Dear Husband"

Mary Writes to Abraham

MAY 1848

"MY DEAR HUSBAND" IS MARY LINCOLN'S TERM OF ADDRESS IN THIS only surviving pre-presidential letter to Abraham. This warmly comports with all else we know of her feelings for him, at least when she was not enraged at him for a) being late to dinner, b) dressing poorly, or c) traveling the legal circuit for nearly half the year.

Why were Mary and Abraham writing letters at this point? Simply, because boardinghouse life in Washington for their young family proved to be unpleasant for all. So Mary took the boys back to her father's house in Lexington, Kentucky. She joined Abraham on part of his speaking tour that fall in New England on behalf of Whig presidential aspirant Zachary Taylor and brought the boys, who were now age five and two. They all returned to Springfield, Illinois, by way of Niagara Falls and the Great Lakes. Their younger son Eddy was sick the next fall and winter, and then died in February 1850.

Evidence of darker years for Mary is already present in this 1848 exchange. Abraham asks her, "Will you be a *good girl*?" referring to her spending habits and her difficulties in getting along with other residents at the boardinghouse, some of them his Whig colleagues in Congress. Conversely, she mentions that one of her former suitors, Edwin Webb, lived nearby in Kentucky, so she intended to visit and "carry on quite a flirtation, you know *we* always had a *penchant* that way." ∽

Mary Lincoln's seal

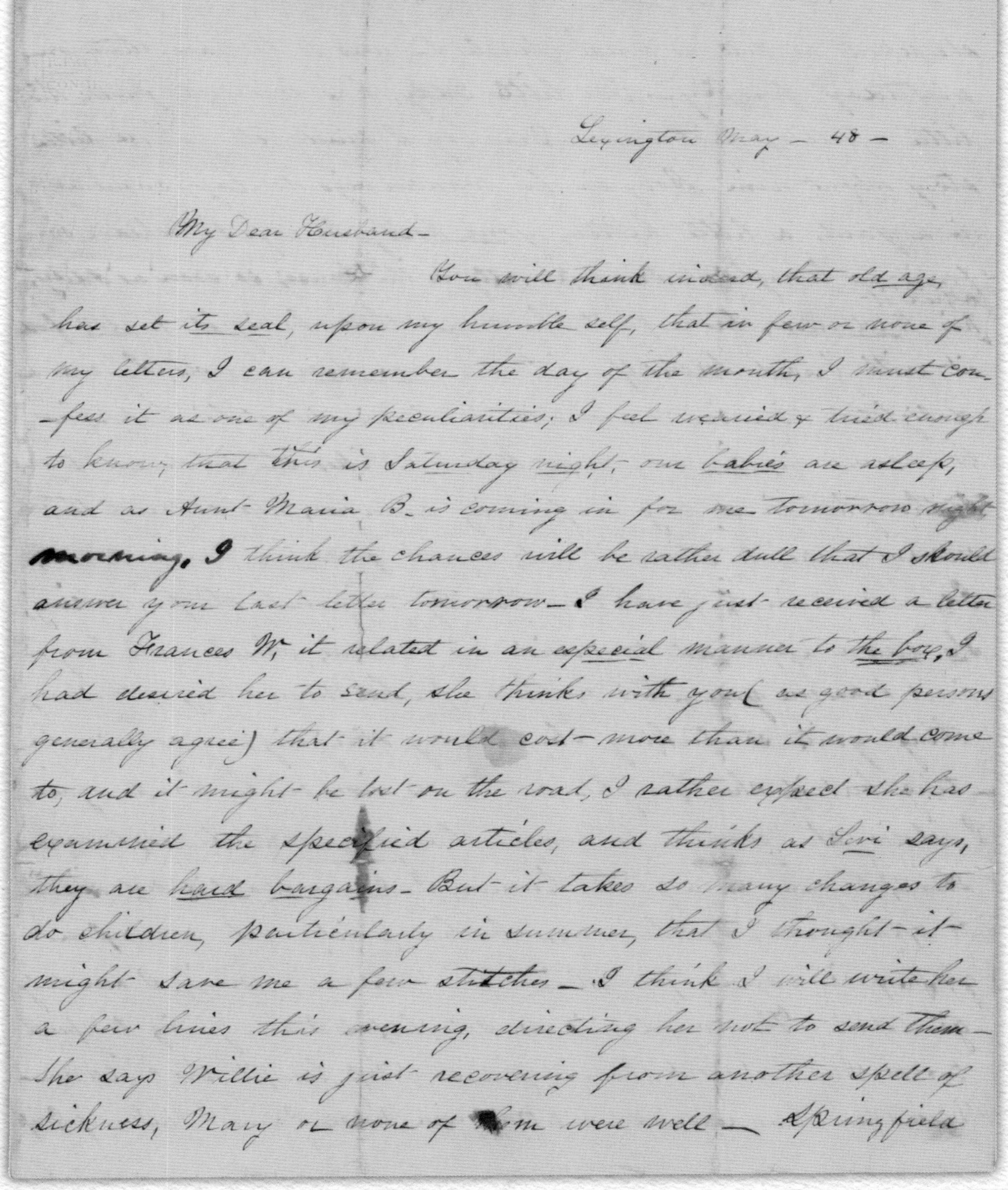

Lexington May — 48 —

My Dear Husband —

You will think indeed, that old age,
has set its seal, upon my humble self, that in few or none of
my letters, I can remember the day of the month, I must con-
-fess it as one of my peculiarities; I feel wearied & tired enough
to know, that this is Saturday night, our babies are asleep,
and as Aunt Maria B— is coming in for me tomorrow ~~night~~
morning, I think the chances will be rather dull that I should
answer your last letter tomorrow — I have just received a letter
from Frances W. it related in an especial manner to the boy, I
had desired her to send, she thinks with you (as good persons
generally agree) that it would cost — more than it would come
to, and it might be lost on the road, I rather expect she has
examined the specified articles, and thinks as Levi says,
they are hard bargains — But it takes so many changes to
do children, particularly in summer, that I thought it
might save me a few stitches — I think I will write her
a few lines this evening, directing her not to send them —
She says Willie is just recovering from another spell of
sickness, Mary or none of them were well — Springfield

ABRAHAM LINCOLN'S YEARS IN SPRINGFIELD WERE SOME OF THE happiest and most fulfilling of his life. It was there that he built a thriving law practice, met and married Mary Todd, raised a family, served part of his four terms in the Illinois legislature, bought his first and only house, and learned of his election as president of the United States. Lincoln's home life was not unlike that of other people. He got ready for work, played with his children, and enjoyed time sitting by the fireplace with his wife.

Three objects in the ALPLM's collection that capture the ordinary aspects of the extraordinary man are his soap dish, gavel, and candle-snuffer. The octagonal soap dish is from Abraham Lincoln's bedroom. It is made of china and most likely lay on a dresser or table next to a pitcher and washing basin, perhaps made of the same or similar material. It is easy to imagine Lincoln's rather large hand sliding a bar of wet soap into the dish as he washed off the dust and dirt from the day.

The gavel, while never owned or used by Lincoln, is actually an integral part of his story, as it was carved by Springfield resident William Duffield from the wood of a tree planted by Abraham Lincoln in the front yard of their Springfield home. The American elm seedling was planted in 1844 by Lincoln, the same year he and Mary purchased the simple Greek Revival or Georgian-style home. The wood became available to Duffield in 1906 after the tree toppled, falling victim to a severe storm, some sixty-two years after Lincoln planted it.

A third object representative of his everyday life in Springfield is the Lincolns' candle-snuffer. Crafted in a barber scissors–like fashion, the candle-snuffer is made of iron. It is the type typically used to snuff out the flame or trim the wick of a candle. By that candle's light, Lincoln might have been reading *Macbeth*, one of his favorite plays. More than a century and a half after his tragic death, the now rusted candle-snuffer stands eerily symbolic, a metaphor for the martyred president and Shakespeare's words:

Out, out, brief candle!
Life's but a walking shadow, a poor player,
That struts and frets his hour upon the stage,
And then is heard no more . . . ⌾

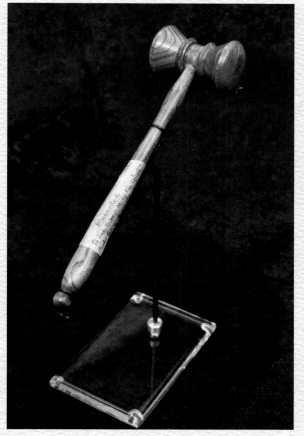

13 "I Give You My Heart"

Mary's Diamond Pendant

1862

ABRAHAM LINCOLN MET HIS FUTURE WIFE, MARY TODD, IN SPRING-field in 1839. Their courtship took place over a two-year period during which they were engaged not once, but twice. (Abraham inexplicably broke off their first engagement in December 1840.) The couple finally married on November 4, 1842. Abraham and Mary were devoted to each other despite the stormy moments in their marriage. They had their share of tragedies, most notably the death of two children, Eddy who died just shy of his fourth birthday in 1850, and Willie who was eleven years old when he died in 1862. Still, their devotion to one another was without question.

Abraham was not one to be caught up in appearances, but he knew Mary appre-ciated the finer things in life, and this may have informed his decision to give her a diamond pendant from the renowned jeweler Tiffany & Co. The gold pendant, given to Mrs. Lincoln during her husband's presidency, is heart-shaped with a pear-cut cen-ter diamond, and twenty-eight smaller diamonds set around it. Lincoln family lore says that when Abraham gave the pendant to Mary, he lovingly pledged, "I give you my heart." The pendant was not the first item from Tiffany that Abraham had given to Mary. In 1861 in commemoration of his first inauguration, Abraham gave her a matching set of jewelry consisting of a seed pearl bracelet, earrings, necklace, and brooch. While the diamond pendant is part of the ALPLM's collection, the inaugural jewelry set belongs to the Library of Congress.

Tiffany also manufactured a special commemorative pitcher in honor of Lincoln's first inauguration. And it was Tiffany that supplied the Union army with cavalry saber swords and surgical instruments. Even after his death, Tiffany continued to be linked to Lincoln when the jeweler was called upon to revise the appearance of the Medal of Honor, which was created during the Lincoln presidency. The newly designed version of the Medal of Honor became known as the Tiffany Cross (see pages 128–29).

What is unique about the Tiffany heart-shaped diamond pendant is not its com-position or beauty, but rather the family story that accompanies it. We know Lincoln as the man who ended the Civil War, saved the Union, abolished slavery, was politically savvy, and so on, but the pendant reveals an often hidden side of Lincoln, the romantic side. He may have given his duty to his country, but he gave his heart to his "Molly."

Remnants from the Second Term

The Family's Private Service

1865

14

As a rail-thin man who did not place much emphasis on meals and grew up eating on plates made of clay or wood, it must have been something of an adjustment for President Lincoln to dine on the finest porcelain of the day. Unlike the formal presidential service, which was purchased early in the first term of the Lincoln presidency, the French Limoges porcelain buff-ground service shown here was purchased late in 1864 after Lincoln was elected to a second term.

While a greater number of pieces of the formal presidential service exist today, the Lincolns' everyday china is rarer and more difficult to find. Mary Lincoln, who was known to spend beyond her means, probably purchased the service from China Hall, a Philadelphia-based store, after she was assured of her husband's re-election and continued salary. Pieces of the service in the ALPLM's collection consist of a soup tureen and cover, a covered vegetable dish, and six matching *pôts de crème* or custard cups, also with covers. The gold-edged bands extend around the circumference of the top of the tureen, as well as the individual pôts de crème, joining nicely together with the same bordering buff bands which extend around the circumference of the bottom of each one's cover. The shape of the tureen is that of an urn with handles formed in the shape of shells. The crown of the cover is topped with a finial in the shape of an artichoke upon which may be found the initial "L" written in Gothic style, designating it as part of the family's private service. The tureen would be used to serve a variety of soups and stews made daily in the White House kitchen, such as mock turtle soup or oyster or terrapin stew, popular meals of the day also served at state occasions. The pôts de crème, in true French tradition, might contain a scrumptious, mouthwatering flavored crème, such as Neopolitane, Chateaubriand, or perhaps the more traditional chocolate or vanilla, any of which undoubtedly appealed to Mr. Lincoln's sweet tooth. Tragically, the Lincolns did not have use of the buff service for very long owing to the president's assassination, which occurred shortly after the new service arrived at the White House. ∞

15

Unlucky Thirteen

Mary Lincoln, Forger

FEBRUARY 1865

MARY LINCOLN NEVER WROTE HER NAME AS "MARY TODD LINCOLN," nor "Mary T. Lincoln." She signed herself thirteen different ways after her marriage in 1842, most often as "Mary Lincoln" or as "Mrs. Abraham Lincoln."

Two of those thirteen ways, sadly, were as "Mary Cuthbert" or "Mrs. Cuthbert." There are fourteen surviving telegrams or letters from 1864–65 that bear one of those forged names, or perhaps it is more polite to call them *noms de guerre*. Mary Lincoln's war on her own indebted identity took as its main prisoner the real Mary Ann Cuthbert, a maid in the White House. Her identity as the sender of the correspondence was employed to cover up or forestall payment of huge amounts of debt from personal overspending by the first lady.

The Cuthbert letters were revealed in 2006. Thus, they are not printed in the 1972 edition of Mary Lincoln's correspondence, nor does Jean Baker's 1987 admiring biography of Mary Lincoln even mention them. In 1994, portions of Senator Orville Browning's diary (R-IL), suppressed upon publication in the 1920s, were also released, with his nearly definitive statements and other evidence about Mary Lincoln's stealing and indebtedness.

Mary wrote the first Cuthbert letter in January 1865, nine weeks after Lincoln's successful 1864 re-election bid. Mary was suddenly frantic, because Philadelphia and New York merchants now demanded payment on a backlog of unpaid bills. Lincoln's renewed twenty-five thousand dollar annual salary ought to make a dent in it, each creditor thought. Apparently not all creditors were aware of the other creditors, though rumors must have circulated in merchant circles. None of them seems to have known that Mary Lincoln owed about twenty-six thousand dollars in early 1865.

When her husband died in April, her income from him ended. The last surviving Cuthbert letter was dated May 18, 1865, a few days before Mary moved out of the White House and assigned various friends to press Congress as well as the merchants to help her. The secret was mostly kept for another year or two, and a public subscription to help her in general eventually netted her nearly eleven thousand dollars in May 1866. Some merchants likely were never fully repaid, or paid at all.

The real Mrs. Cuthbert was found pleading on the steps of the Capitol in 1867 to a senator who had to listen to the tale of how Mrs. Lincoln had taken part of her salary back then, and on occasion, her identity. ∞

Owing to her bad spending habits, Mary Lincoln had considerable debt. To cover up or forestall payments to her creditors, she took on the identity of White House maid Mary Ann Cuthbert.

16

"3 Years, 10 Months, and 18 Days"

The Life and Death of Eddy Lincoln

1846–1850

IT IS SAID THAT NO PARENT SHOULD EVER HAVE TO BURY A CHILD. Sadly and tragically, during their lives together Abraham and Mary Lincoln had to bury two.

Edward Baker Lincoln ("Eddy"), born in 1846, had been named after Abraham's close friend, Edward D. Baker, an attorney who had served with Lincoln in the Illinois House of Representatives and was later Oregon's first US senator. A somewhat sickly child, Eddy Lincoln died in February 1850, about a month before his fourth birthday. He was a victim of consumption, more commonly known as tuberculosis.

Eddy Lincoln's tombstone is cut from off-white limestone and probably no taller than the toddler it memorializes. It has a peace dove engraved at its top and declares that Edward Baker Lincoln lived a brief "3 years, 10 months and 18 days." Engraved at its base is the phrase, "Of such is the kingdom of Heaven," a reference to the biblical verse Matthew 19:14, "Suffer little children, and forbid them not, to come unto me: for such is the kingdom of heaven."

Upon Eddy's death, a service was held in the Lincoln home, presided over by Reverend James Smith of the First Presbyterian Church in Springfield, Illinois. Eddy was buried in Springfield's Hutchinson's Cemetery. Abraham, although not as outwardly distraught as Mary, was affected by the loss of his son, writing to his stepbrother John D. Johnston in February 1850, "We lost our little boy. He was sick fifty-two days & died the morning of the first of the month . . . We miss him very much." No doubt it was the loss of Eddy and other loved ones, including his son Willie who later died in the White House in 1862, which gave Lincoln the courage, insight, and compassion to write some twelve years later to a teenage Fanny McCullough on the loss in battle of her father, William, who was also a friend of Lincoln's: "In this sad world of ours sorrow comes to all . . . you cannot now believe that you will ever feel better. But this is not true. You are sure to be happy again." Referring to the world as a "sad" place, Lincoln revealed his melancholic nature rooted in a life of tragedy and sorrow.

Years later, when Eddy was reburied with his father and brother Willie in the Lincoln Tomb at Oak Ridge Cemetery, the backside of his tombstone was reused by his extended maternal family, who engraved the "Edwards" name on it. ◯◯

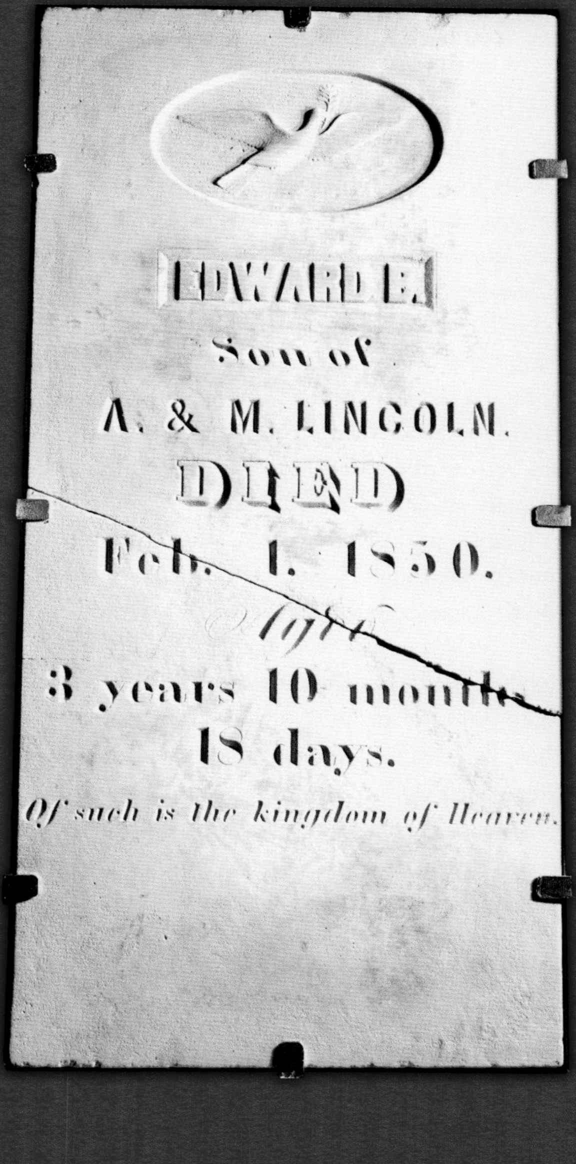
EDWARD B.
Son of
A. & M. LINCOLN.
DIED
Feb. 1. 1850.
Aged
3 years 10 months
18 days.
Of such is the kingdom of Heaven.

Science or Faith?

The Mystery of Abraham Lincoln

1850–1851

LINCOLN'S SON ROBERT WAS BORN WITH STRABISMUS, WHICH MEANT he was cross-eyed, a condition often "cured" in those days by bad home remedies. By evidence of this document, Lincoln took Bobby to the Peoria Eye Infirmary and Orthopaedic Institution when he was seven or eight years old so that Dr. E. S. Cooper could cut a muscle under the eye socket's skin and let the eyeball naturally straighten itself. Cooper had learned a surgical technique for fixing a child's crossed eyes and launched the Peoria Eye Infirmary and Orthopaedic Institution in 1851. Pictured here is the only known copy of his October 27, 1851, circular letter—what we call junk mail today.

The "orthopaedic" part of Cooper's plan meant that the same muscle-cutting at the ankle of a child born with clubfoot had the same curative effect. Lincoln signed his name to testify to the effectiveness of Dr. Cooper's technique (if you look closely at the thirty-odd signatures, you see Lincoln's name at the top of column two). Also supporting Dr. Cooper were Judge David Davis, Senator Stephen A. Douglas, future congressman William Kellogg, most of the other doctors in Peoria, and several non-Illinoisans.

In the same twelve-month period, Lincoln and little Bobby rode 140 miles to a folk-medicine woman in Terre Haute, Indiana, where she rubbed a madstone over a dog bite Bobby had received to draw out rabies—in case that dog had been rabid. Judge Joseph Gillespie of Madison County, Illinois, is our source for this story. He was a skeptic of such "superstition" as performed by the country people from whom Lincoln sprang, yet Lincoln was "fully impressed with" such people's "belief in their virtues from actual experiment." While Lincoln did not presume to know anything further of "the properties of medicines," little Robert grew to be a great attorney and businessman. He died in 1926, rabies-free. We suppose that the dog died much earlier, also rabies-free.

Here, at the midpoint of the nineteenth century was the mystery of Abraham Lincoln, believing in the curative power of a regurgitated lump of calcified cud from a cow, or willing to put his boy's eyeball under the knife. ∽

Peoria Eye Infirmary and Orthopædic Institution.

Dear Sir:

This establishment is just completed, and in readiness as a permanent place, for the reception of all Patients afflicted with *Eye Diseases* as well as those wishing to undergo operrations for the removal of all varieties of *Deformities.*

The building is in a beautiful and a healthy location on the western border of the City of Peoria, where Patients can have comfortable Rooms, Boarding and Nursing, according to the demands of each case.

Every instrument and apparatus calculated to fulfill the designs of such an Institution is provided, and in the Orthopedic Department, several entirely new ones are used, some of which in the Club-foot of young children, frequently obviates the necessity of operating by the knife.

For further particulars, address,

E. S. COOPER, M. D., Peoria, Ill.

Peoria, Ill., October 27, 1851.

Hon. A. LINCOLN,

REFERENCES.

Major F. VORIS,
J. C. FRYE, M. D.,
R. ROUSE, M. D.
JOHN HAMILTON, M. D.
A. G. OSBUN, M. D.
N. S. TUCKER, M. D.
WM. R. HAMILTON, M. D.   *Peoria, Ill.*
A. SEIPMAN, M. D.
E. M. COLBURN, M. D.
Rev. W. B. LINELL,
Rev. H. G. WESTON,
Rev. ADDISON COFFEY,
Hon. E. A. HANNEGAN, U. S. Senator, *Covington, Ia.*
Hon. WILSON SHANNON, Ex-Gov., *St. Clairsville, O.*
Hon. WM. McMURTRY, Lieut. Gov., *Henderson, Ill.*
Hon. DAVID DAVIS, *Bloomington, Ill.*
Gen. A. GRIDLEY,   "   "
Gen. M. K. ALEXANDER, *Paris,* "
Hon. JOHN MOORE, *Springfield,* "

Hon. A. LINCOLN, *Springfield, Ill.*
Hon. S. H. TREAT,   "   "
Hon. T. L. DICKEY, *Ottawa,* "
Hon. WM. KELLOGG, *Canton,* "
Hon. ISAAC P. WALKER, *Milwaukie, Wis.*
Hon. WM. C. BRYANT, Ex-Chief Justice of Oregon,
                           Rockville, Ia.
Hon. JOHN G. DAVIS,   "   "
Bishop L. L. HAMLINE, *Schenectady, N. Y.*
Prof. CHAS. A. POPE, M. D., *St. Louis, Mo.*
Prof. J. B. JACKSON, M. D., *New Orleans.*
Prof. J. MILLER, *Mettamora, Ill.*
JULIUS MANNING, Esq., *Knoxville, Ill.*
JOSIAH McROBERTS, Esq., *Joliet,* "
His Excellency, JOSEPH A. WRIGHT, *Indianapolis, Ia.*
Hon. S. A. DOUGLAS, *Chicago, Ill.*
J. TENBROOK, M. D., *Paris,* "
J. REED, M. D., *Terrehaute, Ia.*
J. SPAULDING, M. D. *Victoria, Ill.*

18 A Birthday Invitation

Willie Lincoln Turns Seven

1857

ABRAHAM AND MARY LINCOLN LOVED TO PAMPER THEIR CHILDREN. This invitation Mary wrote out to Isaac Diller, a playmate of the Lincoln boys, for Willie's seventh birthday party, in 1857. Birthday parties were just beginning to become common at the time, and by the latter 1850s the Lincolns were doing well financially. On their street of a dozen homes lived many more than a dozen boys and girls, of whom several were also invited.

Little Isaac can be seen in the foreground of a photograph of the Lincoln Home taken in summer 1860, where Abraham and his two younger sons (and, hidden behind the fence-corner, their dog Fido) pose for a cameraman (see page 39). Isaac remained in their lives to some extent. As an adult, he became a temperance advocate, like Lincoln. His parents had the great sense to save this invitation, even in the year before Lincoln had run for the Senate against Douglas, though a year after he had received a few nomination votes to be vice president on the new Republican ticket headed by John C. Fremont. Many of the children who attended Willie's party recalled in later years how Mr. Lincoln would carry them on his shoulder down the street, roughhouse with them on the grass, buy them candies on the square, or, once, angrily scold them for using a rope to make a dog do a somewhat painful trick.

Other neighbor children remained "in the Lincoln circle." Little Josie Remann married Albert Edwards, one of Mary Lincoln's nephews. Mary's niece, Mary Jane Wallace, who lived on the next block, married one of the Bakers who ran the Republican newspaper so favorable to Lincoln. Sadly, Willie Lincoln never had the chance to form adult relationships with these people. He died at age eleven in the White House, and his good friend Edward Rathbun, who lived directly across the street, died three years after that, whereupon Mary Lincoln wrote her last letter ever to Edward's mother Hannah. ∞

Willie Lincoln will
be pleased to see you,
Wednesday Afternoon at 3
O'clock.
Tuesday Dec 22d

Isaac Diller

19 At Home in Springfield

A Father and His Sons

1860

WHILE MANY FORMALLY POSED STUDIO IMAGES EXIST OF ABRAHAM Lincoln at various stages in his lifetime, very few semi-candid images exist, particularly any of the Lincoln family's years in Springfield, Illinois. Two of the prized photographs in the ALPLM's collection are 1860 images of Abraham Lincoln with his sons Willie and Tad standing in the front yard of their home on 8th Street.

The images were taken by pioneering photographer John Adams Whipple, who contributed to the development of the daguerreotype. He might also be considered one of the world's first paparazzo, as he camped, albeit with permission from the president, across the street from the Lincoln home to capture these relaxed moments. Whipple's photographs provide a rare glimpse into the everyday home life of Abraham Lincoln and his family. A doting father, Lincoln can be seen standing with his sons Willie and Tad (Tad hidden by a fence post) just inside the white picket fence that formed the perimeter of his property, as passersby look on. The photo has an easygoing feel. It is important not only because it shows Lincoln as family man, but because it shows how readily accessible he was to any and all of his fellow Springfielders, most of whom he viewed as dear friends. It is easy to get lost in the photo as you gaze upon it, wondering what Lincoln, the father, might be saying to his young sons. Might he be telling them a joke as he so loved to do? Letting them know that lunch or dinner would soon be served and urging them to go inside and wash their hands? Commenting on the neighbors passing by, or on Mr. Whipple the photographer from Boston? This is Lincoln pre–Washington, DC, pre–Civil War. This is Lincoln the candidate as "normal" American. ∽

My friends—no one, not in my situation, can appreciate my feeling of sadness at this parting. To this place, and the kindness of these people, I owe everything.
    —Abraham Lincoln, "Farewell to Springfield"

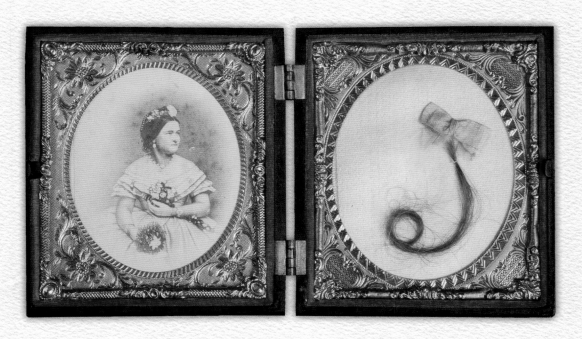

Family Keepsakes

Locks of Love and Affection

1860s

THREE OF THE MOST INTIMATE ARTIFACTS IN THE ALPLM's COLLECtion are individually framed albumen print photographs of Abraham, Mary, and their third son Willie. Each photograph is accompanied by a lock of the person's hair tied with a ribbon. Abraham and Willie's locks are tied with black ribbons, while Mary's is tied with pink, suggesting these might have been *re*framed by or for Mary after the deaths of both her husband and son—Willie, who was eleven years old when he died on February 20, 1862, and Abraham, who died at the age of fifty-six on April 15, 1865. Willie was nine years old when this particular photograph was taken in Springfield at the end of 1860.

The images and locks of hair are set in small mid-nineteenth-century gutta-percha cases with gilt-tin mat. Gutta-percha, made from the sap of a species of Asian tree, was in popular use at the time. It was a customary gesture in this time period to take a clipping of a beloved's hair as a keepsake or remembrance. Abraham's lock of hair is all the more special because it provides for us a tangible piece of the man. To be able to view an actual lock of Lincoln's hair gives the opportunity to see a physical natural remnant of a man who will continue to captivate and inspire people the world over for generations to come. ◌

21 The Little Soldier

Tad's Toy Cannon and Company K Photo Album

1863

ABRAHAM LINCOLN LOVED CHILDREN AND DERIVED GREAT PLEASURE from his own. He was not a strict disciplinarian and frequently gave his boys the full run of his office. This was particularly true of Tad. After Willie's death, the Lincolns showered much attention on the boy, as he was the only Lincoln child still living with his parents while Robert was pursuing a degree at Harvard.

Two items in the ALPLM's collection that show the level of concern and commitment Lincoln had for his young son are Tad's toy cannon and his Company K Photo Album. After Willie's death, Lincoln was particularly concerned about Tad. The president wanted to give something special to the boy, who was attracted to the military and spent much of his young life around the soldiers of the 150th Pennsylvania Volunteer Regiment, Company K, which guarded the White House during most of the Civil War. This resulted in two gifts. The first was a patent-model cannon from Captain John A. Dahlgren, commander of the Washington Navy Yard. The president asked Dahlgren to give Tad, "a little gun that he cannot hurt himself with." To ensure Tad's safety, Dahlgren bent part of its firing mechanism to disarm it. Made of brass and sitting upon a wooden gun carriage made of oak, it has a barrel twelve inches long and less than two inches wide, while the carriage is about nine inches long by six inches wide. It weighs about ten pounds.

The other gift was a photo album, put together by the hundred men of Company K. The members were individually photographed at famed photographer Mathew Brady's studio in Washington, DC. The album is covered in black velvet with brass trim, along with four brass military leaf clusters, one in each corner. Centered on the cover is a brass crest with the inscription:

> Presented
> to
> Tad Lincoln
> by
> Co. K, 150th Pa. V.

The album opens in a horizontal fashion. It is easy to imagine young Tad opening it time and again, viewing the photos of the soldiers he had come to know as a young lad in the White House. These were trusted soldiers who had become trusted friends. ◌

22 Calm in the Storm

The Missing Son

JULY 14, 1863

As if the huge numbers of killed, wounded, and missing soldiers of 1863 were not enough to make the Lincolns despair, their own son Robert went missing for a brief time. A junior at Harvard could be expected to do so now and again, but when he did during the New York draft riots, what parent would not panic?

As father and husband Lincoln usually downplayed drama or the unknown, at least in the sense that he did not want another person to needlessly share his worries. When, for example, Mary was injured in a horse-drawn carriage accident in Washington on July 2, 1863, Lincoln remained calm. As the episode reached many newspapers the next day, he sent a telegram to Robert at Cambridge that read, "Your mother very slightly hurt by her fall," which was true enough at the time. When her head wound became infected (and some have pointed to this moment as the beginning of her personality change and mental decline), Lincoln was more blunt. He instructed Robert, who was now in New York, to come home. Robert did not reply for three days.

By July 14 Lincoln's mood was grievous, and publicly so, about General Meade's failure after Gettysburg, ten days before, to pursue Lee. "If I had gone up there, I could have whipped them myself," he said to John Hay and others present.

All this chronology is much clearer in hindsight, but July 11 was the day the new Conscription Act went into force in New York City, with hundreds of draftees' names appearing in the newspapers on the following day. Over the course of four days the city was aflame with arson and murder directed against blacks (and a Mohawk Indian mistaken for one), Republicans, newspaper offices, and passersby.

We may surmise, without reading Lincoln's mind, that the blows of mid-July 1863 struck him from all sides—as commander-in-chief, as a person committed to civil law, as a husband, and as a father. Without knowing the exact state of the telegraph lines or offices, we may also say that Robert got to the train somehow and reached Washington late on July 14 or early on July 15.

On July 15, with Mary and Robert both safely back at home, Lincoln issued a Proclamation of Thanksgiving, for the nation to mark the twin victories at Gettysburg and Vicksburg. Truly he had much to be thankful for. ∽

Washington, D.C., July 14 6 1863

Rob. T. Lincoln
New York.
5th Av. Hotel.

Why do I hear no more
of you?

A. Lincoln

Robt T. Lincoln. 1861

23 Mansion Politics

"Shoe Tad's Horse"

April 7, 1864

IT SHOULDN'T HAVE BEEN TOO MUCH FOR THE PRESIDENT OF THE United States to be able to walk out the door of the Executive Mansion, cross the lawn to the stables, and request that a blacksmith shoe his son's horse. It is when the timing of the boy's demand and location of the job itself both dim the father's moral lights. Not if he was the first Republican president, or the first non-Democratic president in eight years. Appointments to the largest house in Washington, nearly in the nation, were mainly in the hands of a Democratic Congress. Approximately half of the clerks in the main departments in Washington were mild or determined secessionist sympathizers.

As a result, the Lincolns were expected to pay for about half of their food in the mansion. The other half was provided by assorted government contracts going back some years. Fruits, meats, and bread, yes; vegetables and dairy, no. Servants at their beck and call? Absolutely not. This animus grew when, for example, Mary Lincoln tried to remove someone and replace him or her with someone more manageable. Or when the Republican-dominated Congress began to investigate "secesh feeling" in town after most Democrats seceded in 1860-61.

Coachmen were by necessity a rough lot, and those tending the horses perhaps as much or more so. Thus, when Mary Lincoln fired a stable man in February 1864, and the next night the stables burned—killing Willie's pony and three other horses—Mr. Lincoln knew he was not master of his own yard. He leapt over a hedge to save the pony and wept when others restrained him from the burning pile in hopes of saving the last living possession of the son who had died two years earlier.

If he wanted Tad's horse shoed, it had to be put in writing, on official stationery. Photographic evidence indicates that the job got done, for we can see Tad at the yard's extremity on his South American pony. If only Mr. Lincoln's lesser generals had followed orders so well and sped for southern America with such bravado. ⟳

Shoe Tad's horse for him.

A. Lincoln

April 7. 1864.

24 Some Plank, Some Boy

Tad Builds a Stage

MAY 20, 1864

LUCKY TAD LINCOLN HAD MUCH TO DELIGHT HIM IN HIS DAYS IN THE Executive Mansion. (That is, if you overlook the death of his brother and playmate Willie during their first year there, and his comparative entrapment in a very dangerous city.) It seems that at some point traveling performers came to the Lincolns' home with a puppet show or other small-stage extravaganza, giving the eleven-year-old the fine idea to build a little stage of his own.

The trouble was that he only had at hand the floorboards of his bedroom. Having caused some damage on these, the boy next implored his father to get him additional materials. Usually he did this by bursting into the presidential office, Cabinet meeting

or no, with a smile but no knock. "Papa-day," he might have said, "I want to build a stage."

And so his harried father used official stationery to initiate a chain-of-command. "Mother," he scribbled to Mary, "please put something now in Tad's room." Mrs. Lincoln passed it down (or up?) the chain-of-command, adding, "Please give Tad a board & some plank."

Surely John P. Usher of Indiana, the secretary of the interior, was happy to receive this order, endorse it with his name, and pass it along to Benjamin B. French, the commissioner of public buildings, who held the power to *get things done*. . . .

Mr. French wrote on an envelope, "President, Mrs. Lincoln & Secy. Usher want Tad's room fixed." This he handed to Mr. Halliday, the carpenter. Rube Goldberg and any army private would have appreciated this chain of delegation.

So it was that on May 20, 1864, just one boy commanded five adults. ∽

Will Mr French please fix
up the room of Master Tad
Lincoln as he desires, if it
can properly be done
J P Usher

May 20. 1864
Wrote Mr. Haliday to do the
work Tad wanted and I
would see it paid for
R. B. F.

Executive Mansion,
Washington, _____ , 1864.

Mother— Please put something
now on [   ] [   ]
A.L.

Please give Tad
a board & some
plank
Mrs Lincoln

25

A Dutiful Son

Robert Lincoln's Notes on Burning Letters

1898

PROTECTING ONE'S PRIVACY IS NOT DEEMED UNNATURAL, BUT MANY people are less understanding when the person is world famous. Robert Lincoln knew all of this, yet for his own sake and, more so, the sake of his disturbed mother and his martyred father, he guarded their lives by disposing of family letters. The document shown here lists what was destroyed from 1895 to 1914, which was mostly checks and financial material, but included all the family letters, as well as Mary Lincoln's letters from 1875 to 1876.

A dutiful son, Robert simply repeated what his parents had done. Abraham and Mary burned their letters in 1861 before leaving for Washington. Abraham burned or discarded many other lower-level bits of correspondence too. If Abraham wrote Mary a letter every two weeks during the three to six months he was away from home each year of their marriage, she would have received 150 or 200 letters from him. Let us imagine that between child-minding and house-keeping Mary wrote him forty to eighty letters. Yet only a tiny handful of pre-1861 letters survive—most likely pulled by souvenir-hunters from the burning pile in the Lincolns' backyard.

Historians have for the most part blamed Robert for this activity, mainly because they are eager to read letters from Mary Lincoln's period of madness. Whether for good or ill, some of those did survive, because try as he might, Robert could not locate everything she had written, there being little pattern to it, and because the Lincoln family's notoriety led people to prize, even conceal for generations, the letters they did own.

Robert, like many people, became more interested in his lineage late in life. The result is that many notes and letters about that topic do exist in his papers at the Presidential Library. He saw no reason to preserve his own checks or personal corre-spondence with his wife. In 1898 he was fifty-five years old, essentially done with eight or ten years of public service, and working full time in the private sector, and growing both more private and more involved with protecting his father's privacy. His endless patience in responding to autograph-seekers' queries is probably more remarkable than what he did to shield his mother's insanity from public eyes. ∽

All my family letters
" M. L. letters of 1875-6

NAME OR SUBJECT	REFERENCE MATTER
	Papers burned - in 1895 & after
	All my family letters
	" M. L. letters of 1875-6
	Cheques - 1869-87 incl. 88 - 89 - 90 - 91 & 92
	Rects 1870 " " 88 - 89
	Washington House lease of papers
	Old S & L Docket
	All M. H. Cheques
Dec 98	All Cash books & ledgers except those current
Dec '00	Old Telephone & Gas Co papers
" 03	1897 Ho. repair & alterations receipts
Nov 07	Letters to R & L 1877/1879
May 1911	" " " since to now - except 10 cases of past letters kept
	All Receipts except my late ones
Oct 19 13	All Hiltch building correspondence
"	Lot of old letters to R. L.
Oct 10 14	all that half a dozen old letters to M. L. which came from Chicago
"	all cheques up to 1905

Wishing to protect the privacy of his parents, Robert followed their tradition of destroying family correspondence. He kept a record of his activity leaving future generations to wonder what the contents of the destroyed documents might have been.

Lincoln's fellow attorneys on the circuit: five of the Long Nine

The "Long Nine" was a nickname given to Abraham Lincoln and his eight fellow circuit-riding attorneys, each of whom was at least six feet tall.

PART 2
ATTORNEY

A. Lincoln

Reynolds Jones, 1952, *The Circuit Rider*

26 A Map of the Man

The Map of Huron

May 21, 1836

A map is a window on a place, and an old map can either be a view into the birth of a place or, in some cases, a view of its demise. Lincoln's "Map of Huron" shows the life cycle of a proposed town. It also reveals something important about his personal investments.

For all the emotional and financial hardships Lincoln endured in his New Salem years, he managed to keep afloat. Though a Whig in a town and state of Democrats, the powers-that-be nonetheless got him named postmaster in 1833; a Whig state legislator in 1834; and assistant to the county surveyor, a Democrat. All this could be deemed a school of hard knocks softened by friendly hands. As a surveyor, he platted several short roads, private farms, school sections within townships, and, most colorfully, five entire new towns. The notion of a "paper town" is effectively an American invention, and Lincoln baked his share of that optimistic pie.

Then he wished he had not. Fees for surveying he received, yes. Further income from speculating in new-town lots, no. What is the "explananation"—as he misspelled it in the boxed key to the map—for the town's and his investment failure? A little bit of bad luck, but mainly wrong-headed politics, for which Lincoln was in part responsible. In the same months that he lined out and filed this legally required plat for Huron's projectors, he was pushing as a legislator for state funds to dig a canal that would connect the Sangamon and Illinois Rivers. Eastern states and their watercraft were benefitting from canals hundreds of miles long. Wouldn't a new town on a new canal to the Illinois River make sense?

But the state was overextended just as the Panic of 1837 struck. The crumbling of hopes was a consequence of inflated land prices, Andrew Jackson's death-stab of the Second Bank of the United States, and diversion of canal investment into the railroad. Lincoln might have foreseen some or most of that shift, but his meager savings got him only a couple of cheap town lots at Huron, which within months had become nearly worthless. No canal. No town. No profit. The Map of Huron symbolizes Lincoln's permanent shying away from land. He never again bought land for himself. While others grew wealthy in the 1840s and 1850s, he became only modestly well-off. New towns? He'd rather walk through them than own them. ∽

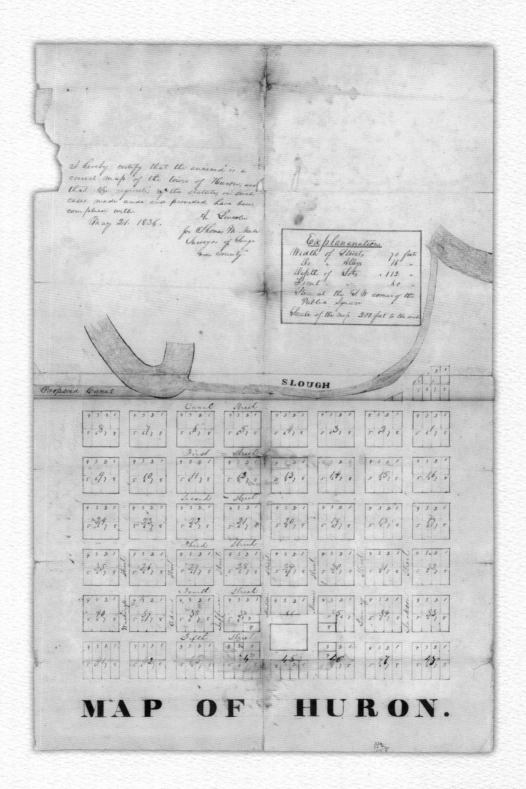

TO THE PUBLIC.

It is well known to most of you, that there is existing, at this time, considerable excitement, in regard to General Adam's titles to certain tracts of land, and the manner in which he acquired them. As I understand, the General charges, that the whole has been gotten up by a knot of Lawyers and others to injure his election; and as I am one of the knot to which he refers, and as I happen to be in possession of facts connected with the matter, I will in as brief a manner as possible make a statement of them, together with the means by which I arrived at the knowledge of them.

Some time in May or June last, a widow woman, by the name of Anderson, and her son, who reside in Fulton county, came to Springfield for the purpose, as they said of selling a ten acre lot of ground lying near town, which they claimed, as the property of the deceased husband and father.—

When they reached town they found the land was claimed by Gen. Adams. John T. Stuart and myself were employed to look into the matter, and if it was thought we could do so with any prospect of success, to commence a suit for the land. I went immediately to the Recorder's office to examine Adams' title, and found that the land had been eatered by one Dixon, deeded by Dixon to one Thomas, by Thomas to one Miller, and by Miller to Gen. Adams. The oldest of these three deeds was about ten or eleven years old, and the latest more than five, all recorded at the same time, and that within less then one year. This I thought a suspicious circumstance, and I was thereby induced to examine the deeds very closely, with a view to the discovery of some defect by which to overturn the title, being almost convinced then it was founded in fraud. I finally discovered that in the deed from Thomas to Miller, although Miller's name stood in a sort of a marginal note on the record book, it was no where in the deed itself. I told the fact to Talbott, the Recorder, and I proposed to him that he should go to Gen. Adams' and get the original deed, and compare it with the record, and thereby ascertain whether the defect was in the original, or there was merely an error in the recording. As Talbott afterwards told me, he went to the General's, but not finding him at home, got the deed from his son, which, when compared with the record, proved what we had discovered was merely an error of the Recorder.— After Mr. Talbott corrected the record, he brought the original to our office, as I then thought an I think yet, to show us

that it was right. When he came into the room, he handed the deed to me, remarking that the fault was all his own. On opening it, another paper fell out of it, which on examination, proved to be an assigment of a judgement in the Circuit Court of Sagamon County, from Joseph Anderson, the late husband of the widow above named, to James Adam's, the judgemeut being in favor of said Anderson against one Joseph Miller.. Knowing that this judgement had some connection with the land affair, I immediately took a copy of it, which is word for word, letter for letter and cross for cross as follows :

"Joseph Anderson,) Judgment in Sangamon Circuit
vs.   ) Court against Joseph Miller obtain-
Joseph Miller.) ed on a note originally 25 dolls and
interest thereon accrued.

"I assign all my right, title and interest to James Adams, which is in consideration of a debt I owe said Adams.
"May 10th, 1827.
"JOSEPH M. ANDERSON.
mark."

As the copy shows, it bore date May 10, 1827; although the judgement assigned by it was not obtained until the October afterwards, as may be seen by any one on the records of the Circuit Court. Two other strange circumstances attended it which cannot be represented by a copy. One of them was, that the date "1827" had first been made "1837" and without the figure "3" being fully obliterated, the figure "2 had" afterwards been made on top of it; the other was that, although the date was ten years old, the writing on it, from the freshness of its appearance was thought by many, and I believe by all who saw it, not to be more than a week old. The paper on which it was written had a very old appearance; and there were some old figures on the back of it which made the freshness of the writing on the face of it, much more striking than I suppose it, otherwise might have been.

The reader's curiosity is no doubt excited to know what connection this assignment had with the land in question. The story is this : Dixon sold and deeded the land to Thomas. Thomas sold it to Anderson ; but before he gave a deed, Anderson sold it to Miller and took Miller's note for the purchase money. When this note became due, Anderson sued Miller on it, and Miller procured an injunction from the court of Chancery to stay the collection of the money until he should get a deed for the land. Gen. Adams was employed as an attorney by Anderson in this chancery suit, and at the October term, 1827, the injunction was dissolved, a judgment given in favor of Anderson against Miller, and it was provided that Thomas was to execute a deed for the land in favor of Miller, and deliver it to Gen.

Adams to be held up by him, till Miller paid the judgement, and then to deliver it to him. Miller left the county without paying the judgement. Anderson moved to Fulton County, where he has since died. When the widow came to Springfield last May or June, as before mentioned, and found the land deeded to Gen. Adams, she was naturally led to enquire why the money due upon the judgement had not been sent to them, inasmuch as he. Gen. Adams, had no authority to deliver Thomas' deed to Miller until the money was paid. Then it was the Gen. told her, or perhaps her son, who came with her, that Anderson, in his life time, HAD ASSIGNED THE JUDGEMENT TO HIM. Gen. Adams. I am now told that the General is exhibiting an assignment of the same judgement bearing date "1828." and in other respects, differing from the one described ; and that he is asserting that no such assignment as the one copied by me, ever existed ; or if there did, it was forged between Talbott and the lawyers, and slipped into his papers, for the purpose of injuring him.— Now I can only say that I know precisely such an one did exist, and that Ben. Talbott, Wm. Butler, C. R. Matheny John T. Stuart, Judge Logan, Robert Irwin, P. C. Canedy, and S. M. Tinsley, all saw and examined it ; and that at least one half of them will swear that IT WAS IN GENERAL ADAMS' HANDWRITING. And further, I know that Talbott swear that he got it out of the General's possession and returned it into his possession again.— The assignment which the General is now exhibiting purports to have been signed by Anderson in writing. The one I copied was signed with a cross. I am told that Gen. Neale, says that he will swear, that he heard Gen. Adam's tell young Anderson that, the assignment made by his father was signed with a cross.

The above are facts, as stated. I leave them without comment. I have given the names of persons who have knowledge of these facts, in order that any one who chooses may call on them, and ascertain how far they will corroborate my statements. I have only made these statements because I am known by many to be one of the individuals against whom the charge of forging the assignment and slipping it into the General's papers, has been made ; and because our silence might be construed into a confession of its truth. I shall not subscribe my name ; but I hereby authorise the editor of the Journal to give it up to any one that may call for it.

Caught, Red-Handed

Lincoln on the Attack

1837

27

THE DOCUMENT SHOWN HERE IS THE OLDEST PRINTED PIECE OF writing by Lincoln. Dating from August 1837, it is apparently the only surviving copy and was not revealed until the 1990s. Its content throws new light on Lincoln's law career, his daring, and his conviction to rectify what he saw as a malfeasance.

Known as the "Adams Handbill," it attempted to prevent the Democrat James Adams from getting re-elected as probate justice of the county. Instead it led to a libel action *Adams v. Logan*, named after Lincoln's later law partner, who pursued the history that Lincoln had discovered, namely, that Adams had doctored the courthouse deed books in 1827 in order to shift an illiterate widow's ten acres of land to himself. The signature (an X) of the widow is seen in column 2, copied by Lincoln as part of the sordid summary. Lincoln kept up the attack when he learned that Adams had been indicted in Oswego County, New York, in 1818 for the same trick. Perhaps this is why Adams had removed to frontier Springfield in 1821?

In the 1830s President Andrew Jackson had so divided the nation by what the Whigs deemed as dictatorial, anti-economic, and non-constitutional actions that fist-fights at the campaign became a common occurrence. When Lincoln's law partner John T. Stuart excoriated Stephen A. Douglas on the platform in a Springfield street in 1838, punches led to ear-biting. (Stuart, the biter, won the seat in Congress.) For Lincoln, a Whig, ideology was part of it; but the Democrat Adams was also a crook, as were others. Yet Lincoln's printing the evidence and posting it around town only three weeks before voting day in 1837 was not enough. In the end, Adams was re-elected probate judge.

Adams reformed, more or less, and soon joined the Mormon Church, rising to a position of leadership. He pursued the libel case against Logan for a time with Douglas as his attorney, and Lincoln opposing—before the suit was dropped. He died in 1843, the same year Lincoln first tried to get his own party's nomination to Congress. Sometimes "progress" just comes from the passing of the old guard, when younger, harder-working people are allowed to rise. ⌘

28

An Embarrassing Mistake

Lincoln Apologizes

FEBRUARY 20, 1849

ON FEBRUARY 20, 1849, THE SAME WEEK IN WHICH HE WAS AWARDED US patent No. 6,469, Lincoln found himself having to write an apology. Some money Lincoln had been asked to deliver to a legal client by a fellow attorney had gone missing. But had it been Lincoln's fault?

Three key things about his character emerge from this single letter. First, that fellow attorney, Charles R. Welles of Springfield, would entrust him to deliver a sum of cash to a client, which was a St. Louis banking firm in this case.

Second, we learn about Lincoln's fairly unusual habit of storing things in his stovepipe hat: "To make it [the envelope with cash] more secure than it would be in my

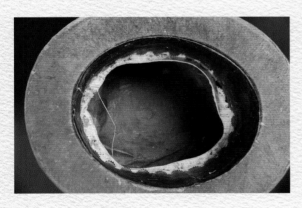

hat, where I carry most all my packages, I put it in my trunk." Evidently, Lincoln forgot about the "trunk" package when he got to St. Louis and delivered only the packages stored in his hat.

Third, when he later found the envelope in his trunk, he entrusted it to a young man he knew who was heading back upriver to St. Louis. That young man, Thomas Yeatman, was the stepson of Senator John Bell of Tennessee, as well as the son-in-law of Lincoln's Springfield friend, US district judge Nathaniel Pope. Yeatman was "of unquestioned and unquestionable character," Lincoln assured Welles, and thus Lincoln supported Yeatman's story that a pickpocket must have seen him take the cash from Lincoln while on the boat, for Yeatman could not recall anything else after the exchange. Lincoln was not only trustworthy; he was trusting and steadfastly stood by Yeatman in the days following the loss of the cash. ∞

To make it more secure than it would be in my hat, where I carry most all my packages, I put it in my trunk.—A. LINCOLN

Washington, Feb. 20. 1849.

C. R. Welles, Esq.

Dear Sir:

This is tuesday evening, and your letter enclosing the one of Young & Brothers to you, saying the money you sent by me to them, had not been received, came to hand last saturday night — The facts, which are perfectly fresh in my recollection, are these; You gave me the money in a letter (open I believe) directed to Young & Brothers — To make it more secure than it would be in my hat, where I carry most all my packages, I put it in my trunk — I had a great many jobs to do in St. Louis, and by the very extra care I had taken of yours, overlooked it — On the Steam Boat near the mouth of the Ohio, I opened the trunk, and discovered the letter — I then began to cast about for some safe hand to send it back by — Mr. Yeatman, George Pope's son-in-law, and step son of Mr. Bell of Tennessee, was on board, and was to return immediately to St. Louis from the Mouth of Cumberland — At my request, he took the letter and promised to deliver it — and I heard no more about it till I received your letter on saturday — It so happens, that Mr. Yeatman is now in this City; I called on him last night about it; he said he remembered my giving him the letter, and he could remember nothing more about of it — He told me he would try to refresh his memory, and see me again concerning it to-day — which, however he has not done — I will

29 Lincoln from A to Z

A Well-Worn Bill-Book

1850

MORE THAN A CENTURY AND A HALF BEFORE FILES WERE STORED ON hand-held flash drives and smartphones, there was something called the bill-book, which was a portable means to keep important documents organized. Much like an oversized wallet with a series of compartments, the bill-book allowed for a systematic filing of documents which, when folded up, could be held in the palm of one's hand. Bill-books like Lincoln's were often carried in cases, coat pockets, or affixed to belts.

It is unknown precisely at what point in his life Lincoln used this now quite distressed looking bill-book. When folded it measures three-and-three-eighths by nine inches. When unfolded, it expands to more than two feet in length. It contains eight separate compartments that would have allowed Lincoln to file his legal briefs, correspondence, bills, calling cards, and the like alphabetically for easy reference. One can only imagine the important documents this bill-book held and how Lincoln filed them. Did he file most of his own personal documents under "A" for Abraham or "L" for Lincoln? Did he file notes from his wife Mary under "M" along with telegrams from George B. McClellan, the general who continually frustrated him? Did G and H overflow with missives from General Ulysses S. Grant, his assistant secretary John Hay, and Vice President Hannibal Hamlin? Did the last compartment hold a bill from Lincoln's chiropodist Issachar Zacharie?

The only remnant found in it was the torn portion of an 1850 legal deed concerning a woman's dower rights in a land transaction from Logan County, just north of Springfield. As for the rest, we will never know for sure, but the bill-book gives ample opportunity for scholars and armchair historians alike to let their minds wander with possibilities. One other thing is certain: The condition of the well-worn bill-book indicates that Lincoln used it frequently. Sometime after her husband's death, Mary Lincoln left the bill-book to her sister, Elizabeth Todd Edwards, who passed it down to her granddaughter Mary Edwards Brown. It was a historic and treasured keepsake of Brown's grand-uncle Abraham, a man she was never able to meet. ◦◦

Elizabeth Todd Edwards

Mary Edwards Brown

30 Working like a Donkey

Lincoln's Law Office Book

1842–1843

MANY OF US HAVE A FIRMLY FIXED IMAGE OF LINCOLN AS A MAN WHO told good stories and practiced a little law before he was launched into the political arena. After a dozen researchers spent two decades studying ninety-eight thousand documents related to about fifty-six hundred legal actions, they determined that Lincoln was just about the busiest attorney in the southern two-thirds of Illinois, and one of the busiest before the state's Supreme Court.

During the twenty-five years Lincoln was nearly a full-time attorney, he argued 331 cases before the state's highest court. The contents of the volume shown here may be obscure to a layman, yet they contain the decisions Lincoln won or lost. Adding drama is the fact that Stephen A. Douglas was a justice on the court in 1841–1842.

The secret of success for an attorney? Don't appear to be too eager for work or acclaim, but work like a donkey when handed the papers. The secret of success for an aspiring politician could reside along similar lines.

Just before this volume was printed, the court ruled that "no book shall be taken from the Library of the Supreme Court, without the consent of the Court." With that established, Lincoln's partner William Herndon wrote his firm's name into this and every law book he and Lincoln owned. There would be no mistaking it for a library book, and no other law office could rightly claim it.

Etching by Kate M. Hall ca. 1915

J. Young Scammon, the court reporter during Lincoln's time there, went on to successfully practice law in Chicago. In June 1865 he hired Robert Lincoln as an apprentice when that young man suddenly had to support his mother and little brother. ∞

Objects of Time

The Lincoln Clocks

1845–1850

WILLIAM SHAKESPEARE, ONE OF LINCOLN'S FAVORITE WRITERS, WROTE: "All the world's a stage, and all the men and women merely players: they have their exits and their entrances; and one man in his time plays many parts. . . ." Lincoln was keenly aware of the stage on which he stood. Over the course of time, he played many parts: president, husband, father, friend, Emancipator, and Union savior. Still, Lincoln understood time was fleeting and his moment on the stage might be brief owing to the number of death threats he received.

Two artifacts which literally exemplify Lincoln's delicate dance with time are his clocks, one from the Lincoln-Herndon law office and the other from his home, both in Springfield, Illinois. The law office timepiece is an American-made, mahogany-cased shelf clock manufactured by Chauncey Jerome of New Haven, Connecticut. Jerome was known for manufacturing affordable mantel clocks and was one of the most famous American clockmakers of the mid-nineteenth century. The law office clock contains a brass timepiece, unique for its day as Jerome's clocks typically were made with wooden timepieces. Jerome's name appears in script on the painted face of the clock along with Roman numerals one through twelve. The clock is of classical form. Just below the face of the clock is a reverse-printed scene of Westminster Abbey fading from view. The tone of the clock is robust as it gongs on the hour. Similarly, the timepiece from the Lincoln home is also a mantel clock, with a painted face, and Roman numerals one through twelve. Floral designs adorn each corner. Just below its face is a reverse-printed scene of a locomotive, with freight and passenger cars attached, belching steam as it exits a tunnel while townsfolk look on. The law office clock is in working order; the home clock is not. The former provides almost a secret moment of intimacy with the dearly departed president when one hears the same tick-tocks, chimes, and gongs Lincoln, his family, or Herndon heard on a daily basis as the seconds, minutes, and hours ticked away. Leo Tolstoy, the Russian author and admirer of Lincoln, once said, "the two most powerful warriors are patience and time." Lincoln certainly understood this, exercised the former, but sadly in the end, was denied the latter. ∞

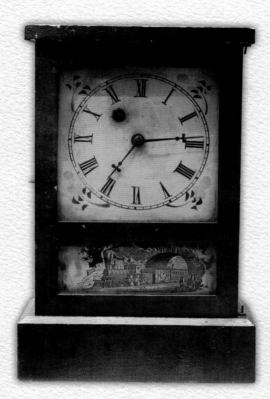

Two mantel clocks used by Lincoln during his Springfield years: one in his home (upper left) and one in his law office (lower right)

32 The Power of Baldwin's Pen

Flush Times *for Abraham Lincoln*

1853

JOSEPH G. BALDWIN WAS A SMALL-TOWN ATTORNEY IN ALABAMA IN the years before the Civil War. He wrote the book that Lincoln could have written for Illinois and Indiana, had the prairie storyteller ever set pen to paper in that vein. Baldwin's effort, published in 1853 by Daniel Appleton Co. of New York as *The Flush Times of Alabama and Mississippi: A Series of Sketches*, found a niche audience around the nation, including central Illinois.

Chapters include such familiar business as rough marriages, "disputin'" over parcels of land, and members of the bar who over-indulge in oyster pie. Henry Clay Whitney of Champaign County, Illinois, is the one who brought Baldwin's book to Lincoln's attention, lending it to him and then enjoying the secondhand pleasure of watching Lincoln read aloud from it to circuit attorneys in the county towns, while they laughed and guffawed. Today the spine still sort of naturally opens to the beginning of the chapter called "Jonathan and the Constable," which is all about a "hoss" thief.

Authorial fame during the war got Baldwin only so far, however. He had moved to California before the fighting began, while his mother remained in her native Virginia. According to a November 1863 letter discovered around 2005 by a retired scholar in Alabama, Baldwin went to the Executive Mansion in hopes of getting a pass over the lines to visit his mother and was being pushed away by a doorkeeper when the president overheard the name. "Baldwin? Joseph Baldwin, of *Flush Times*? C'mon in!" As Baldwin soon reported in so many words to a friend, "We grew very pleasant and spent an hour together . . . very cosily. He . . . knew all about me and more about *Flush Times* (which seems to be one of his classics) than I knew myself. He says he is always quoting me. . . ."

Baldwin then broached the topic of his neutrality in the war and his wish to visit his aged mother over the lines. Lincoln said "no," and thanked him warmly for coming. ⌘

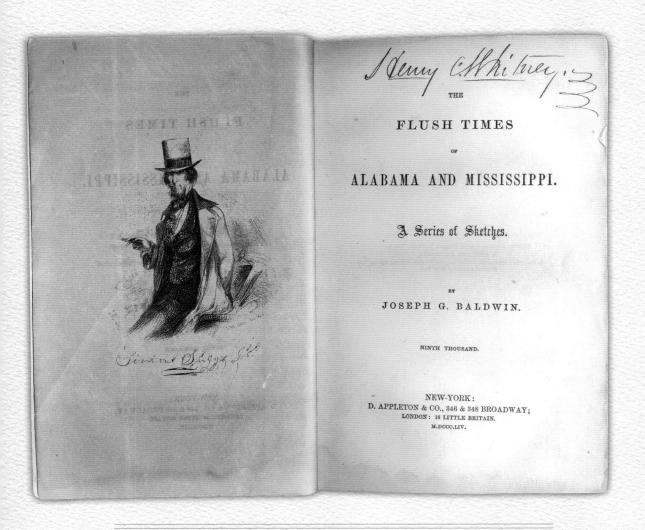

THE

FLUSH TIMES

OF

ALABAMA AND MISSISSIPPI.

A Series of Sketches.

BY

JOSEPH G. BALDWIN.

NINTH THOUSAND.

NEW-YORK:
D. APPLETON & CO., 346 & 348 BROADWAY;
LONDON: 16 LITTLE BRITAIN.
M.DCCC.LIV.

"... *Lincoln read aloud from it* (Flush Times) *to circuit attorneys in the county towns, while they laughed and guffawed.*"

33

Bullock's Addition

Lincoln Represents Aunt Maria

August 4, 1855

In the case of *Bullock v. Viney*, one of Mary Lincoln's aunts, Maria Bullock, was pitted against a man who bought Springfield city lots from her but never paid up. So, Aunt Maria hired Lincoln to settle the tangled matter, which dragged on for more than six years before she recovered her money. This exceptional plat map drawn in 1855 for the case shows her lots as "Bullock's Addition." That area is about a mile west of today's Presidential Museum, and is now opposite Springfield High School. There were many pieces of paper involved in the lengthy court action, but on this particular plat map of August 1855 Lincoln wrote the three lines in the middle, and the six lines at the bottom.

He was working in a familiar circle. Zimri Enos, the surveyor for the map, was an old card-playing friend. James Matheny, the circuit clerk and recorder, had stood as Lincoln's best man at his wedding in 1842. Josiah Francis, the justice of the peace, served in the legislature with Lincoln after starting the Whig newspaper, the *Sangamo Journal*, for which Lincoln often wrote anonymous or pseudonymous pieces.

It could not have been a happy occasion when Lincoln was obliged to visit the site of the unpaid lots. Aunt Maria's land was directly across the street from the City Grave Yard (center, in light blue), which was next to the private cemetery where baby Eddy Lincoln was buried in 1850. ∾

Zimri Enos was the surveyor of the 1855 plat map on which "Bullock's Addition" is drawn.

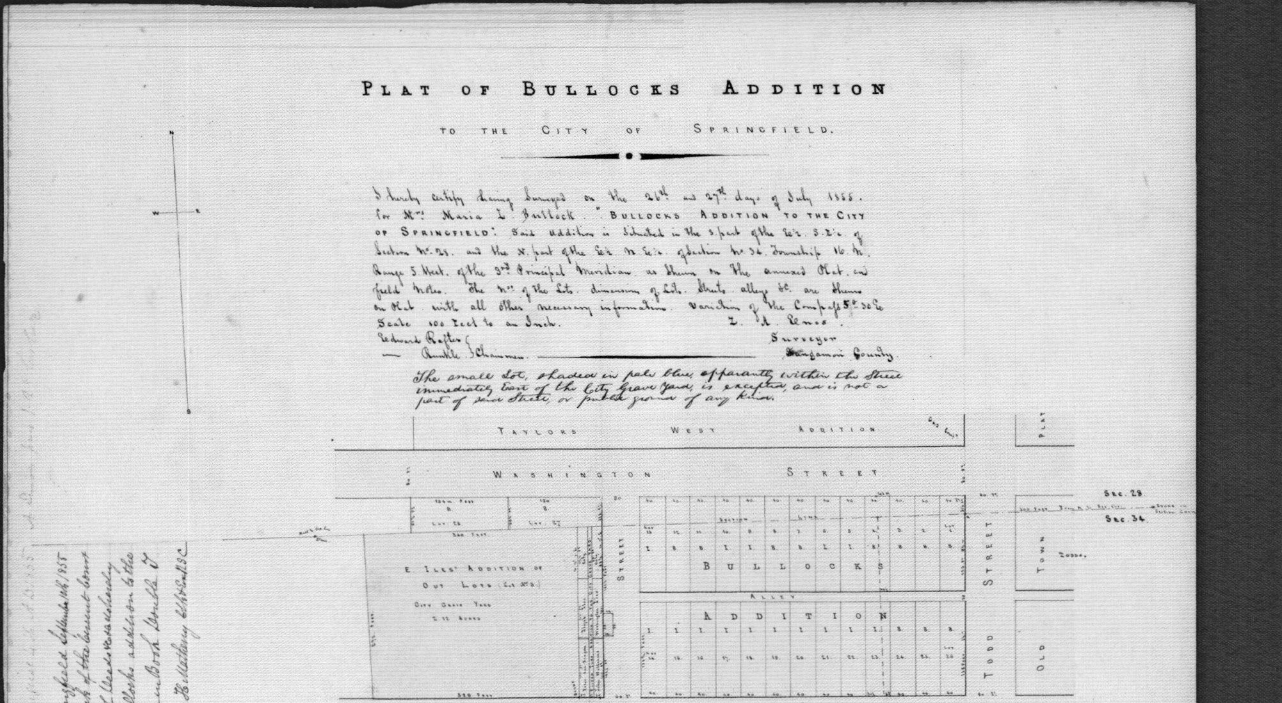

PLAT OF BULLOCKS ADDITION

TO THE CITY OF SPRINGFIELD.

I hereby certify having surveyed on the 24th and 27th days of July 1855, for Mrs. Maria L. Bullock "Bullocks Addition to the City of Springfield". Said addition is situated in the S. part of the S½. S.E. of Section No. 23. and the N. part of the N.E. S½. of Section No. 26. Township 16 N. Range 5 West. of the 3rd Principal Meridian as shown on the annexed Plat, and field notes. the No. of the Lots, dimensions of Lots, Streets, alleys &c. are shown on Plat with all other necessary information.

Scale 100 feet to an Inch.

Z. A. Enos
Surveyor

The small lot, shaded in pale blue, apparently within the street immediately East of the City Grave Yard, is excepted, and is not a part of said Street, or public ground of any kind.

TAYLORS WEST ADDITION

WASHINGTON STREET

E. ILES' ADDITION of Out Lots [Lot No. 2.]

BULLOCKS

ALLEY

ADDITION

TODD STREET

OLD TOWN

ADAMS STREET

EDWARDS + MATHERS ADD'T   WILEYS ADDITION   Lot No. 3. E. ILES' ADDITION of Out Lots.

State of Illinois
Sangamon County SSS

Before me the undersigned an acting Justice of the Peace within and for the county aforesaid, came Mrs. Maria L. Bullock personally known to me to be the same person who proceeded to be made the above Plat of Bullocks Addition to the city of Springfield and the Survey thereon shown, and acknowledged said Plat for the purpose of having it recorded according to law, all which I hereby certify.

Given under my hand and seal, the first day of August A.D. 1855.

Josiah Francis, J.P. SSS

Reflections of the Man

Mr. Lincoln's Mirror

1858–1860

34

ONE OF ABRAHAM LINCOLN'S GREATEST TRAITS WAS HIS SENSE OF humor. He loved hearing or telling a good joke, most especially when the joke was on him. His self-deprecating humor made him all the more likable. Consider once when a detractor called him two-faced. Lincoln responded, "If I had two faces, would I be wearing this one?"

As is well known, Abraham Lincoln was a man more concerned with substance than appearance. After an eleven-year-old girl named Grace Bedell suggested that he let his "whiskers grow" for in her opinion "all the ladies like whiskers and they would tease their husbands to vote for you," Lincoln responded, "As to the whiskers, having never worn any, do you not think people would call it a piece of silly affect[at]ion if I were to begin it now?" Clean-shaven or whiskered, Lincoln used his mirror and, as a man of honesty and high integrity, had no problem looking into it. The mirror in the ALPLM's collection is a portable shaving mirror Lincoln used while riding the 8th Judicial Circuit late in his Illinois career. Made from lightly stained oak, it could be folded and neatly tucked away in its self-contained wooden, rectangular box-of-a-case. When the case faced Lincoln in a vertical fashion, he could unlock it and gently lift the lid at which point the mirror, hinged to the top front of the case, would fold down and rest upon the edge of the bottom front of the case. Handmade around 1859 by Ben Carr, a farmer who lived about twenty miles from Springfield, the glass surface and silver backing of the mirror itself are worn with age. And while it is now as much opaque in spots as it is reflective, its owner remained ever thus—reflective. If Abraham Lincoln's mirror could talk, it might tell us what no photograph, painting, or life-mask could reveal as the face and countenance of the man changed with each passing moment of his life; with each passing piece of legislation; each battle, each death of a child. ∞

35 Peace-Making Lawyer

The Non-Litigious Lincoln

MARCH 3, 1859

MR. HADEN KEELING MUST HAVE BEEN IRATE. THREE TIMES HADEN, his father, and his siblings had lost small lawsuits in which the firm of Lincoln & Herndon was involved. It seems the Keelings' paperwork was never quite orderly enough for the court.

In 1859 Haden built a cellar for a man who paid up, but something was wrong again in Keeling's contract. That seems to be the origin of the famous note to the right. Keeling moved to Canton, Illinois, from Springfield, and pursued the suit. Lincoln advised against it. By the time Keeling ignored the advice and ended up in the state Supreme Court, Lincoln was packing to move to Washington, and William Herndon took up the suit at Keeling's insistence. Keeling lost again.

How many such characters had Lincoln met in his quarter-century at the law? Was Keeling ornery, sloppy, or just unlucky? Lincoln was practicing the advice he had jotted down as notes for a law lecture, which he may never have delivered: "Discourage litigation. Persuade your neighbors to compromise whenever you can. Point out to them how the nominal winner is often a real loser—in fees, expenses, and waste of time. As a peacemaker the lawyer has a superior opportunity of being a good man. There will still be business enough."

The attorney-president operated from the principle that exiting from a prickly situation with a small loss of honor was preferable to losing money and perhaps the verdict—the "whole game" as he dubbed it during the Civil War.

The timing of something else Lincoln certainly wrote in the same year also sheds light on his mindset. His "Lecture on Discoveries and Inventions" reveals the method and logic and concision of expression that we see in short form in the letter to Keeling. The odds that Keeling ever heard this lecture, delivered five or six times in public, are sadly slim, just as his bank account grew slimmer too from not taking Lincoln's advice. ⌇

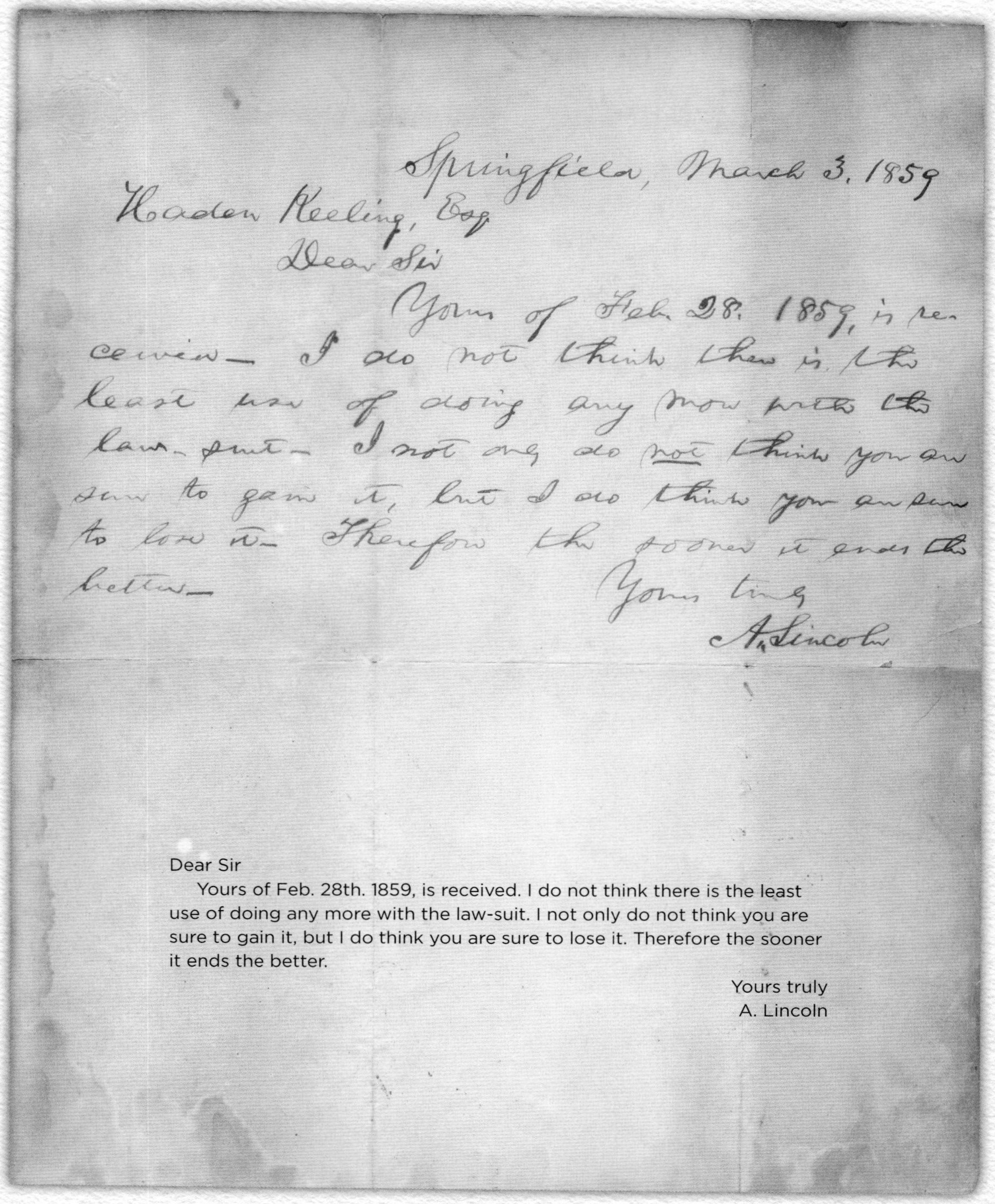

Springfield, March 3, 1859

Haden Keeling, Esq

Dear Sir

Yours of Feb. 28. 1859, is received. I do not think there is the least use of doing any more with the law-suit. I not only do not think you are sure to gain it, but I do think you are sure to lose it. Therefore the sooner it ends the better.

Yours truly

A. Lincoln

Dear Sir

Yours of Feb. 28th. 1859, is received. I do not think there is the least use of doing any more with the law-suit. I not only do not think you are sure to gain it, but I do think you are sure to lose it. Therefore the sooner it ends the better.

Yours truly
A. Lincoln

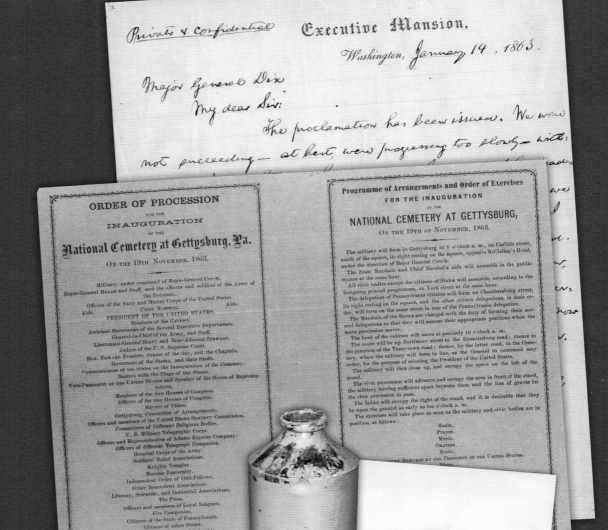

A sample of Abraham Lincoln's stationery while in the White House, commonly called the Executive Mansion at the time; a program for the dedication of the National Cemetery at Gettysburg; an inkwell from Lincoln's law office; and an envelope with President Lincoln's wax seal

PART 3
∾ WORDSMITH ∾

A. Lincoln

Abraham Lincoln's pen

Bass-Ackwards

Spoonerisms of an Unkempt Frontier

CA. 1850

FOR ALL LINCOLN'S REPUTATION AS A HUMORIST AND TALE-TELLER, that aura arose almost entirely from his spoken words. Here is the only humorous tale he ever wrote out, reportedly at the request of a court clerk in 1850 who heard him tell it and wished to have it captured for posterity.

> He said he was riding <u>bass-ackwards</u> on a <u>jass-ack</u>, through a <u>patton-cotch</u>, on a pair of <u>baddle-sags</u>, stuffed full of <u>binger-gred</u>, when the animal <u>steered</u> at a <u>scump</u>, and the <u>lirrup-steather</u> broke, and throwed him in the <u>forner</u> of the <u>kence</u> and broke his <u>pishing-fole</u>. He said he would not have minded it much, but he fell right in a great <u>tow-curd</u>; in fact, he said it give him a right smart <u>sick</u> of <u>fitness</u>—he had the <u>molera-corbus</u> pretty bad. He said, about <u>bray dake</u> he come to himself, ran home, seized up a <u>stick</u> of <u>wood</u> and split the <u>axe</u> to make a light, rushed into the house, and found the <u>door</u> sick abed and his <u>wife</u> standing open. But thank goodness she is getting right <u>hat</u> and <u>farty</u> again.

What Lincoln is doing here is stringing one spoonerism after another. He's deliberately switching the initial letters of contiguous words; the milieu is the unkempt, uncensored frontier. Lincoln was a man's man, the legal circuit was a man's world, the voters were men, and the listeners were nearly all men. ∞

. . . he was riding bass-ackwards on a jass-ack, through a patton-cotch . . .
—A. LINCOLN

He said he was riding <u>bass ackwards</u> on a <u>jass-ack</u>, through a <u>patton-cotch</u>, on a pair of <u>baddle-sags</u>, stuffed full of <u>binger-gred</u>, when the animal <u>steered</u> at a <u>scump</u>, and the <u>lirrup-steather</u> broke, and throwed him in the <u>forner</u> of the <u>kence</u>, and broke his <u>pishing fole</u>. He said he would not have minded it much, but he felt right in a great <u>tow-curd</u>; in fact, he said it give him a right smart <u>sick of fitness</u>— he had the "<u>molera-corbus</u>" pretty bad— He said, about <u>bray dake</u> he came to himself, raw home, seized up a <u>stuck</u> of <u>wood</u> and split the <u>axe</u> to make a light, rushed into the house, and found the <u>door</u> sick abed, and his wife standing open— But thank goodness she is getting right <u>hat</u> and <u>farty</u> again—

37 Little Pamphlet, Big Effect

The "House Divided" Speech

June 16, 1858

THE FAME OF LINCOLN'S "HOUSE DIVIDED" SPEECH ON JUNE 16, 1858, to launch his Senate campaign against the incumbent Stephen A. Douglas, belies one aspect of its printing history. Many newspapers printed the speech the next day or week, and soon most people could read the seven face-to-face debates that occurred between August 21 and October 21 because dozens of papers across the nation printed them. Those printers first out of the gate to get pamphlet versions of the "House Divided" speech into stores did not fare so well. There are, for example, no known individual printings of most of those seven debates; the newspapers did the trick, or the 1860 book version refreshed memories of the issue that was not going away: the wrongness of slavery.

Each of the "House Divided" pamphlets pictured here is the only copy catalogued in any library. No copies have been sold at public auction that we know of, though conceivably a private collector or two owns one or both of these.

O. P. Bassett of Sycamore takes the crown for "first off." He ran the Republican newspaper in that northern Illinois town, and his printed pamphlet of Lincoln's speech remains all on one sheet, uncut, with half the pages printed upside down for the folding-and-slicing machines. In 1983 the Presidential Library issued a facsimile reprint of this unique item.

As for the German edition, some immigrants had already become too southern, or so it seems. Their views, to the limited extent that we have ethnic polling figures from that time, more or less mirrored the broader public's: They were divided about slavery. Lincoln did not win enough of their votes in 1858 to prevail over Douglas, but he did win enough of their votes in 1860 to prevail over Douglas, Breckinridge, and Bell. This version of the 1858 speech, printed in Alton, Illinois, includes the Republican platform as well as an abridged version of a speech the same day by Gustav Koerner, the leading German-American politician in the state. This goes to show that a little pamphlet for a little group can have a big effect. ⌀

EVENING JOURNAL TRACTS, NO. 7.

REPUBLICAN PRINCIPLES.

SPEECH

OF

HON. ABRAHAM LINCOLN,

OF ILLINOIS,

AT THE

REPUBLICAN STATE CONVENTION, HELD AT SPRINGFIELD, ILLINOIS, JUNE 16, 1858.

If we could first know *where* we are, and *whither* we are tending, we could then better judge *what* to do, and *how* to do it.

We are now far into the *fifth* year, since a policy was initiated, with the *avowed* object and *confident* promise of putting an end to Slavery agitation.

Under the operation of that policy, that agitation has not only *not ceased*, but has *constantly augmented*.

In *my* opinion, it *will* not cease, until a *crisis* shall have been reached and passed. "A house divided against itself cannot stand." I believe this government cannot endure permanently half *slave* and half *free*. I do not expect the Union to be *dissolved*. I don't expect it will cease to be divided. It will become *all* one thing, or *all* the other. Either the *opponents* of Slavery will arrest the future spread of it where the public mind shall rest in the belief that it is in course of ultimate extinction; or its *advocates* will push it forward till it shall become alike lawful in *all* the states, *old* as well as *new*—*North* as well as *South*. Have we no *tendency* to the latter condition?

Let any one who doubts, carefully contemplate that now almost complete legal combination—piece of *machinery* so to speak—compounded of the Nebraska doctrine, and the Dred Scott decision. Let him consider not only *what work* the machinery is adopted to do, and *how well* adopted; but also, let him study the *history* of its construction, and trace, if he can, or rather *fail*, if he can, to trace the evidences of design, and concert of action, among its chief bosses, from the beginning. But, so far, *Congress* only, had acted; and an *indorsement* by the people, *real* or *apparent*, was indispensable, to *save* the point already gained, and give chance for more. The new year of 1854 found Slavery excluded from more than half the states by state constitutions, and from most of the national territory by congressional prohibition. Four days later commenced the struggle, which ended in repealing that congressional prohibition.

time the war broke out, Lincoln had the leisure, as well as the patriotism, to join one of the volunteer companies which was formed in the neighborhood of New Salem. To his unbounded surprise and satisfaction, he was chosen captain by his fellow-soldiers. The place of rendezvous was at Richland, and as soon as the members of the company met, the election took place. It was expected that the captaincy would be conferred on a man of much wealth and consequence among the people, for whom Lincoln had once worked. He was a harsh and exacting employer, and had treated the young man, whom everybody else loved and esteemed, with the greatest rigor; a course which had not increased his popularity. The method of election was for the candidates to step out of the ranks, when the electors advanced and joined the man whom they chose to lead them. Three-fourths of the company at once went to Lincoln; and when it was seen how strongly the tide was set in his favor, the friends of the rival candidate deserted him, one after another, until he was left standing almost alone. He was unspeakably mortified and disappointed, while Lincoln's joy was proportionably great.

The latter served three months in the Black Hawk war, and made acquaintance with the usual campaigning experiences, but was in no battle. He still owns the lands in Iowa that he located with warrants for service performed in the war.

An incident of the campaign, in which Lincoln is

*"William Kirkpatrick"— I never worked for him— L.

concerned,* illustrates a trait of his character no less prominent than his qualities of integrity and truth. One day an old Indian wandered into Lincoln's camp, and was instantly seized by his men. The general opinion was that he ought to be put to death. They were in the field for the purpose of killing Indians, and to spare the slaughter of one that Providence had delivered into their hands was something of which these honest pioneers could not abide the thought. It was to little purpose that the wretched aborigine showed a letter signed by General Cass, and certifying him to be not only a model of all the savage virtues, but a sincere friend of the whites. He was about to be sacrificed, when Lincoln boldly declared that the sacrifice should not take place. He was at once accused of cowardice, and of a desire to conciliate the Indians. Nevertheless, he stood firm, proclaiming that even barbarians would not kill a helpless prisoner. If any one thought him a coward, let him step out and be satisfied of his mistake, in any way he chose. As to this poor old Indian, he had no doubt he was all that the letter of General Cass affirmed; he declared that they should kill *him* before they touched the prisoner. His argument, in fine, was so convincing, and his manner so determined, that the copper-colored ally of the whites was suffered to go his ways, and departed out of the hostile camp of his friends unhurt.

* The authority for this anecdote is Mr. William G. Green, a tried and intimate friend of Lincoln during early manhood.

Correcting History

Lincoln Edits His Biography

38

WHEN HE WAS TWENTY-THREE YEARS OLD, WILLIAM DEAN HOWELLS was collared to ghostwrite a campaign biography of Lincoln in 1860. He did a good job, in light of the fact that he never met with the candidate and previously had authored only a single book of poems. Follett, Foster & Co. from Howells's home town of Columbus, Ohio, wanted a book about the lanky Illinoisan to sell alongside its edition of the 1858 Lincoln-Douglas Debates—a volume Lincoln himself edited scrupulously for March 1860 publication just in case he won the Republican Party's presidential nomination.

Howells set to work putting the second-ever Republican candidate for president in a good light. Lincoln was more or less content with the result, which was officially titled *Lives and Speeches of Abraham Lincoln and Hannibal Hamlin* and released to the public in the late summer.

Samuel Parks, a legal-circuit friend of Lincoln's, bought a copy of the book in July. He did not think that every word of it sounded right, so being a lawyer he sent it to the candidate himself for review. Perhaps he knew that Lincoln had written "I authorized nothing" about the biography to Ohio Republicans even though he was willing to help a young writer. Possible embarrassment to the party from inaccurate phrasing was Lincoln's main worry. Indeed, a lie that Douglas had told during the 1858 debates about the Republican platform had made its way into the original Howells book.

Lincoln read the pages containing his biography and speeches and penciled in his corrections. He then returned the volume to Parks.

In 1938 the Abraham Lincoln Association issued a facsimile edition of the biographical pages, so that one may see Lincoln's pencil changes. What Lincoln wrote is now taken to be absolutely true, and what he did *not* change is mostly taken to be true.

There are many different versions of the book, published in different cities and containing different text, but there is only this one carefully improved by Lincoln. Howells, meanwhile, went on to write more than one hundred other books. ⌘

39

"The Better Angels of Our Nature"

First Inaugural Desk and Inkwell

1861

By the time Abraham Lincoln sat down in Springfield at his brother-in-law Clark Smith's desk in January 1861 to write his First Inaugural Address, he had already delivered a number of his well-written and memorable speeches. One was his president-making 1860 Cooper Union Address wherein he encouraged those in attendance, "Let us have faith that right makes might, and in that faith, let us, to the end, dare to do our duty as we understand it." Another was his address to the 1858 Republican State Convention in which he proclaimed, "A house divided against itself cannot stand." When it came to writing speeches, he had already raised his own bar to a considerable height, in some respects writing himself into the American presidency.

As he prepared his First Inaugural Address, he knew his words must be persuasive and confident in order to stave off war and keep more of the southern states from seceding while also entreating states that had already seceded to return to the Union. This was as consequential a speech as any he had ever written, and it required a single-minded focus without distractions. Smith provided Lincoln the refuge he sought with a private office complete with desk, chair, and inkwell. The massive walnut desk has a gently sloped writing surface and numerous pigeon-holes for storage. And while the inkwell Smith provided was ordinary enough—a common inkwell made of wood, painted with an eagle, standard issue for the day—it ceased to be ordinary the moment in January 1861 when Lincoln began to use it. How long the president-elect toiled at the desk is uncertain, but the hours he spent at it produced some of the most vivid and impassioned words Lincoln had ever written:

> In your hands, my dissatisfied fellow-countrymen, and not in mine, is the momentous issue of civil war. The Government will not assail you. You can have no conflict without being yourselves the aggressors. You have no oath registered in heaven to destroy the Government, while I shall have the most solemn one to "preserve, protect, and defend" it. We are not enemies, but friends. We must not be enemies. Though passion may have strained it must not break our bonds of affection. The mystic chords of memory, stretching from every battlefield and patriot grave to every living heart and hearthstone all over this broad land, will yet swell the chorus of the Union, when again touched, as surely they will be, by the better angels of our nature. ∞

40 Lincoln's Longest

The Conkling Letter

AUGUST 26, 1863

ABRAHAM LINCOLN WAS NOT ALLOWED TO VOTE WHILE PRESIDENT. His residence was officially Springfield, and though he might have considered going back home in the fall of 1862 to boost support for Illinois Republicans that season, he did not. Just as well, because his first boss John Todd Stuart became a Democrat and ran for Congress that year against Leonard Swett, a Lincoln operative, and won. Democrats won a majority in both chambers of the Illinois legislature. The Emancipation Proclamation was not popular in Illinois, or Indiana, or various other places.

Time and victories change opinions. Gettysburg, Vicksburg, and other Union advances in 1863 helped, yet Lincoln was still unsure whether his safety or his cause would be enhanced by visiting home. He was invited to speak at a meeting of Unconditional Union men in Springfield on August 31. He wrote, instead, his longest known "letter" to friend James C. Conkling, on August 26, 1863, for Conkling to read out loud at a political gathering. "Read it slowly" was the scant advice Lincoln appended in a private note to Conkling.

At the event, in front of thousands of people split between the parties, the letter seems to have done some good. Over the long term, it proves to be a great piece, a full speech with memorable ideas. "If you will not fight for the negro," Lincoln through Conkling said to dubious townsmen, "they seem willing to fight for you. But no matter. Fight you, then, exclusively to save the Union. I issued the proclamation on purpose to aid you in saving the Union."

Did Lincoln alter a word or phrase to suit the voice of another man? Apparently not. Conkling acted more like a radio transmitter for the president than a medium. Yet we have nothing to compare the Conkling letter against, for Lincoln never before or after served as "speechwriter" for another person to deliver.

The little-advertised connection between the families continued. Mary Todd had been very close to Mercy Levering before they became Mrs. Lincoln and Mrs. Conkling. Then Robert Lincoln (Harvard '64) and Clint Conkling (Yale '63) became soberminded correspondents in later years, Robert in the East relying again on the Springfield man, Clint, for advice and good works back home. Most materially, Clint helped direct Robert's money to install the organ at the new Westminster Presbyterian Church in Springfield in 1915. That had been the parish Robert's parents did *not* attend—the openly antislavery one. Time and victories do help opinions to change. ∞

the broad bay, and the rapid river, but also up the narrow muddy bayou, and wherever the ground was a little damp, they have been, and made their tracks. Thanks to all. For the great republic — for the principle it lives by, and keeps alive — for man's vast future, — thanks to all.

Peace does not appear so distant as it did. I hope it will come soon, and come to stay; and so come as to be worth the keeping in all future time. It will then have been proved that, among free men, there can be no successful appeal from the ballot to the bullet; and that they who take such appeal are sure to lose their case, and pay the cost. And then, there will be some black men who can remember that, with silent tongue, and clenched teeth, and steady eye, and well-poised ~~borne~~ bayonet, they have helped mankind on to this great consummation; while, I fear, there will be some white ones, unable to forget that, with malignant heart, and deceitful speech, they have strove to hinder it.

Still let us not be over-sanguine of a speedy final triumph. Let us be quite sober. Let us diligently apply the means, never doubting that

us— that from these honored dead we take increas=
ed devotion to that cause for which they here gave
the last full measure of devotion— that we here
highly resolve that these dead shall not have
died in vain— that this nation, under God,
shall have a new birth of freedom— and that
government of the people, by the people, for the
people, shall not perish from the earth.

Four score and seven years ago our fathers brou
ght forth upon this continent, a new nation, conceived
in Liberty, and dedicated to the proposition that all
men are created equal.
Now we are engaged in a great civil war, testing
whether that nation, or any nation so conceived, and
so dedicated, can long endure. We are met on a great
battle field of that war. We have come to dedicate
a portion of that field, as a final resting place for
those who here gave their lives, that that nation
might live. It is altogether fitting and proper that
we should do this.
But, in a larger sense, we can not dedicate—
we can not consecrate— we can not hallow—
this ground. The brave men, living and dead, who
struggled here, have consecrated it, far above our
poor power to add or detract. The world will
little note, nor long remember, what we say here, but
it can never forget what they did here. It is for us,
the living, rather, to be dedicated here to the unfin
ished work which they who fought here, have, thus
far, so nobly advanced. It is rather for us to be
here dedicated to the great task remaining before

"Shall Not Perish"

The Gettysburg Address

NOVEMBER 19, 1863

41

THE PERSON WHO MAY HAVE TOUCHED LINCOLN'S HEART AND MIND most directly was William Johnson, the free African American who worked for him in the White House. Lincoln understood that the Fugitive Slave Act of 1850 (he signed its repeal in June 1864) endangered every African American, making women and men alike the targets of slave-nappers seeking reward or dirty-market cash south of the river. William Johnson, who enjoyed the protection and employ of the president of the United States, would not be fully free until all people were free.

Johnson rode with Lincoln to Gettysburg on the train. He brushed his coat, saw that his boots were clean, trimmed his hair and beard, all on the night Lincoln finished writing the Address in a borrowed room. These two men saw and heard the final pen strokes run over the paper. Perhaps each said a prayer before sleep that night, Lincoln in the only one-man bed left in the overcrowded town, Johnson in the stable out back.

The document Lincoln wrote that night and read from on November 19, 1863, probably no longer exists. Its function was to reach the few thousand present and the millions more who would read the transcript the next day and week. The copy pictured here, owned by the Presidential Library since 1944, was written about three months later when it was requested by Edward Everett, the main speaker that morning. The Everett copy is the earliest extant version in Lincoln's hand to include "under God," since those words are not present in the two drafts he later gave to his secretaries in Washington. Lincoln would have hoped that if the war failed, if our politics failed, if our republic failed, then perhaps God would grant some earthly freedom to the non-white. Lincoln did not presume to know God's wishes or intents. But he had worked out in his mind many years prior that slavery was wrong, that William Johnson's life of limbo must be redeemed somehow.

Abraham Lincoln and his clearer vision passed to us a timeless desideratum, yet dated from a poetically mathematical four score and seven years before (that is, from 1776) that "all men are created equal." The phrase went from Thomas Jefferson's pen into the Declaration of Independence—which is also available in essentially every language on earth. ∞

42

Compiling History

Edward Everett's Notebook

1864

THE UNITED STATES OF AMERICA HAS LONG CELEBRATED ITS GREAT orators, from Patrick Henry and Daniel Webster to Henry Clay and Edward Everett. And while oration is still a skill practiced and appreciated today, it has changed much since the eighteenth and nineteenth centuries when orators would think nothing of delivering a speech hours in length. Such was the case on November 19, 1863, at the dedication of the new National Cemetery at Gettysburg, Pennsylvania.

The cemetery committee had selected the great orator from Massachusetts, Edward Everett, to give the keynote address. Abraham Lincoln was asked to follow Everett, with "a few appropriate remarks." Everett spoke for two hours, giving a brilliant oration laying out the circumstances that brought together the gathered crowd, the honored dead, and the nation on that mournful day. Lincoln then delivered his "few" points about the cemetery itself—his Gettysburg Address—as he was asked to do. His now immortal speech lasted some two minutes, about which Everett later wrote, "I should be glad, if I could flatter myself that I came as near to the central idea of the occasion, in two hours, as you did in two minutes."

In January 1864, Everett asked Lincoln to write out his remarks so he could add it to the notebook he was putting together for a charity auction. Proceeds from the sale of the notebook would benefit wounded Civil War soldiers and their families. It was apparently the first time Lincoln wrote out the Address since his delivery of it some three months earlier. The notebook, now in the ALPLM's collection, is approximately two inches thick from cover to cover—a testament to the bulk of Everett's speech, plus notes, photos, and maps occupying fifty-five pages—in sharp contrast to Lincoln's mere two pages. Interestingly, for as much as Everett recognized the brilliance of Lincoln's remarks, he made no reference to them on the cover. Of further interest is the fact that Everett refers to his own remarks as the "Address" and to Lincoln's remarks as a "dedicatory speech." In the end, the "Gettysburg Address," as it has been known now for generations, describes Abraham Lincoln's remarks, not Everett's. ∞

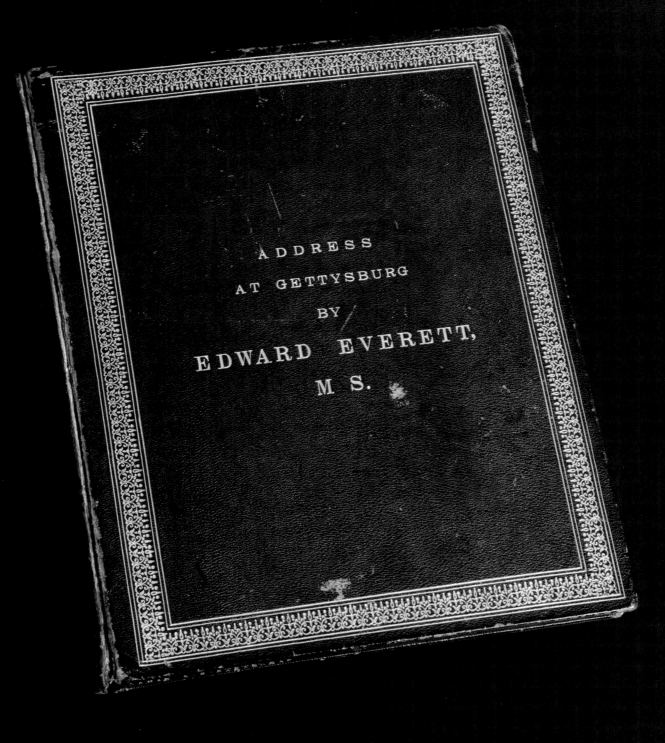

ADDRESS

AT GETTYSBURG

BY

EDWARD EVERETT,

M S.

43 Letter to Mrs. Amanda Hall

Hopes and Principles for Wartime America

MARCH 20, 1865

VERY RARELY WAS LINCOLN PROUD OF HIMSELF. YET ON A FEW OCCA-sions he was pleased enough with what he had written to fulfill requests for copies of things such as the Gettysburg Address and any excerpt from the Second Inaugural Address.

There are five excerpts that Lincoln penned of the Second Inaugural Address of March 4, 1865, thanks to a few individuals' immediate sense of what is now a general public perception: that it was a magnificently eloquent statement of his hopes and principles for wartime America and a postwar world.

Pictured here is the result of one of those five requests. (Another slightly shorter one sold at auction in October 2015 for $1.7 million.) What surprises some is that the passage perhaps most quoted these days, the final paragraph beginning "With malice toward none; with charity for all," is not what Lincoln chose here in this longest of his self-excerpts. Rather, he chose the most religiously grounded section:

> Fondly do we hope—fervently do we pray—that this mighty scourge of war may speedily pass away. Yet, if God wills that it continue until all the wealth piled by the bondman's two hundred and fifty years of unrequited toil shall be sunk, and until every drop of blood drawn with the lash shall be paid by another drawn with the sword, as was said three thousand years ago, so still it must be said: "The judgments of the Lord are true, and righteous altogether."

The opening couplet is among Lincoln's most beautiful utterances. The rest anchors him in the Judeo-Christian tradition as firmly as anything he wrote or said, bringing Lincoln's belief in the ultimate Providence of the Lord into play from Psalm 19, verse 9 up to the year AD 1865.

Amanda Hall was the daughter of a pioneer minister in Michigan, and the sister of a new congressman from that state, Thomas Ferry, whom Lincoln had barely met. Before we think that Mrs. Hall had an inside track to Lincoln, those other fortunate few who received excerpts were much more politically tied to Mr. Lincoln through his Cabinet or through war-work. We must assume that he wrote to her from the heart, as he did to all people in the full speech. ⌘

Executive Mansion,

Washington, March 20. , 1865

Mrs. Amanda H. Hall

Madam

Induced by a letter of yours
to your brother, and shown me by him, I send you what
follows below.

Respectfully,

A. Lincoln

"Fondly do we hope— fervently do we pray— that this mighty
scourge of war may speedily pass away. Yet, if God wills, that it
continue until all the wealth piled by the bondman's two hundred and fifty years of unrequited toil shall be sunk, and
until every drop of blood drawn with the lash shall be
paid by another drawn with the sword, as was said
three thousand years ago, so still it must be said;

"The judgments of the Lord are true, and righteous altogether."

Abraham Lincoln

44

"Mortality"

Lincoln's Favorite Poem

1865

ABRAHAM LINCOLN LOVED READING AND WRITING POETRY. WE SEE this first with his cypher book (see pages 6–7).

He actually published two poems, *The Bear Hunt* and *My Childhood Home I See Again*, during his lifetime. Of course, Lincoln's flair for the poetic was never more evident than in the rhythmic prose of his Second Inaugural Address:

> *Fondly do we hope,*
> *fervently do we pray,*
> *that this mighty scourge of war*
> *may speedily pass away.*

There is no doubt that Lincoln loved lyrical language, and he was apt to admit of "feeling a little poetic this evening." Lincoln read the poetry of Robert Burns and Edgar Allan Poe, but it was a less-known Scottish poet, William Knox, who garnered the honor of having written Abraham Lincoln's favorite poem, "Mortality," which is also known as "Oh! Why Should the Spirit of Mortal Be Proud?"

Knox's work is almost a prophetic statement about the president who loved it so. A little-known artifact in the ALPLM's collections is a broadside produced in 1865 that contains the poem. The broadside was printed in Philadelphia by song publisher A. W. Auner, who did this as part of the national tributes to the martyred president. It bears a woodcut of the Great Seal of the United States at the top.

In addition to the broadside, the ALPLM has some original books of poetry and magazines owned by Mary Lincoln, which were undoubtedly read by both her and her husband. Some of these include an 1860 edition of Lord Byron's *Gallery of Byron Beauties*; Thomas Gray's *Elegy Written in a Country Churchyard*; a two-volume set of the works of Henry Wadsworth Longfellow; and a four-volume set of the work of Edgar Allan Poe that Robert Lincoln bought in 1862.

Even in death, Lincoln and poetry are inextricably linked, and many a poet has used him as the subject, most notably in "O Captain! My Captain!," from Walt Whitman's *Leaves of Grass* and "On a Poem by Lincoln: 'My Childhood Home I See Again'" by former poet laureate Billy Collins. ❧

PRESIDENT LINCOLN'S

FAVORITE POEM,

Oh! why should the spirit of mortal be proud?
Like a swift, fleeting meteor, a fast-flying cloud,
A flash of the lightning, a break of the wave,
He passeth from life to his rest in the grave.

The leaves of the oak and willow shall fade,
Be scattered around and together be laid;
And the young and the old, and the low and the high,
Shall moulder to dust and together shall lie.

The infant and mother attended and loved;
The mother that infant's affection who proved,
The husband that mother and infant who blessed,
Each, all, are away to their dwellings of rest.

The hand of the king 'that the scepter hath borne;
The brow of the priest that the mitre hath worn;
The eye of the sage and the heart of the brave,
Are hidden and lost in the depths of the grave.

The peasant, whose lot was to sow and to reap;
The herdsman, who climbed with his goats up the steep;
The beggar, who wandered in search of his bread,
Have faded away like the grass that we tread.

So the multitude goes, like the flower of the weed,
That withers away to let others succeed;
So the multitude comes, even those we behold,
To repeat every tale that has often been told.

For we are the same our fathers have been;
We see the same sights our fathers have seen;
We drink the same stream and view the same sun,
And run the same course our fathers have run.

The thoughts we are thinking our fathers would think;
From the death we are shrinking our fathers would shrink;
To the life we are clinging they also would cling;
But it speeds from us all like a bird on the wing.

They loved, but the story we cannot unfold;
They scorned, but the heart of the haughty is cold;
They grieved, but no wail from their slumber will come;
They joyed, but the tongue of their gladness is dumb.

They died; aye! they died; we things that are now,
That walk on the turf that lies over their brow,
And make in their dwellings a transient abode,
Meet the things that they met on their pilgrimage road.

Yea! hope and despondency, pleasure and pain,
We mingle together in sunshine and rain;
And the smile and the tear, the song and the dirge,
Still follow each other, like surge upon surge.

'Tis the wink of an eye, 'tis the draught of a breath,
From the blossoms of health to the paleness of death;
From the gilded saloon to the bier and the shroud,
Oh! why should the spirit of mortal be proud?

A. W. AUNER, SONG PUBLISHER, Cor. 11th & Market, Philada.

45

"A Heap of Jokes"

Wiggo Meets the Whittler

WIGGO T. SCHERR, A DANISH IMMIGRANT, WROTE HIS GRANDSON Elliott a six-page letter in 1912 to share his recollections of working in Springfield in the 1840s. In it, he recounted, "When not too busy or absent on circuit, [Mr. Lincoln] was almost daily in our store . . . a jovial, full of fun man, a heap of jokes. . . . had a penchant for whittling. If [he] could get a piece of soft pine, out came his knife and at it he went. In court while most lawyers made notes, he with his retentive memory did not seem necessary to use these, but if could get a nice pine stick, soon had a nice pile of shavings about him."

Later on Lincoln told a White House visitor, "I always used a cane when I was a boy. . . . My favorite one was a knotted beech stick, and I carved the head myself." Perhaps forgotten today is how commonly, in Lincoln's and Wiggo Scherr's day, a man and his penknife did battle with bits of wood.

Mr. Scherr died a few months later. He thereby captured for his grandson, and for everyone else since, a unique portrait that supports other tales of how often Lincoln whittled, how the furniture in the Sangamon County courthouse was nicked and scratched from Lincoln's and other attorneys' fidgety penknives. Perhaps most of all, we ought to try to remember Lincoln as his neighbors and voters remembered him—an amusing man, friendly to all, leavening his cares about family, law, politics, or history with a story or two. Much good can come from writing letters to the younger generation, or telling them jokes. ∽

A whittled-grip walking stick originally from the collection of Lincolniana collector Benjamin Richardson, friend of Mary and Tad Lincoln

My dear Elliott:

Have your letter of 4th inst. It gives me sincere gratification to see your good hand writing. I hope you'll continue to improve and eventually make an A1. scribe. While do not want to find fault, want to ask you to make some changes, particularly in the "lower case" (as printers call small type) you make r "r" this looks careless; a failing we are all apt to get into as advance in age. easiest corrected in youth. In regard to your inquiry as to Prest. Lincoln. I left St. Louis Saturday, April 30th 1847 at 5 A.M. by stage route — then no Railroad — arriving at Springfield Ill. between 1 and 2 O'clock Sunday morning. about 21 hours. I was to be employed by James L. Lamb. (Some day if spared to see you will give particulars) From your question I infer you think Mr. Lincoln was a young man, he had wife and some children, "Tad" a lad I think 6 or 7 and "Bob" probably your age. Mr. Lincoln was then quite a prominent lawyer, was Mr. Lamb's Attorney. When not too busy or absent on circuit, he was almost daily in our store, hence got quite familiar with him, a jovial, full of fun man, a heap of jokes. There are too many of his peculiarities for me to write, but one he had was a penchant for whittling, if could get a piece of soft pine, out came his knife and at it he went. In court while most lawyers made notes, he with his retentive memory did not seem necessary to use these, but if could get a nice pine stick, soon had a nice pile of shavings about him.

heap of jokes.

PART 4
∽ Candidate ∽

A. Lincoln

46

Dirt under His Nails

Lincoln Breaks the Prairie

August 24, 1860

DURING HIS PRESIDENTIAL RUN IN 1860, LINCOLN WROTE THIS LET-
ter to his mother's first cousin John Hanks. He did so because during the campaign
John's brother Charles, an avowed Democrat, had questioned Lincoln's actual farming
and rail-splitting experience while exaggerating his own supposed closeness to Lincoln.

Thus Lincoln wrote about Charles that after more of the extended family moved
to Illinois in 1830, "I helped him at breaking pra[i]rie, with a joint team of his and
ours, which in turn, broke some on the new place we were improving." Lincoln was also
quite sure that he had never even met Charles until the late 1820s. After this point, no
one seems to have questioned Lincoln's dirt-under-the-nails youth.

Would it have mattered in the campaign if they had? How accustomed to rough-
hewn seekers of the presidency was the American electorate by 1860? Less than we
might now think. Some candidates—William Henry Harrison in 1840, Lewis Cass
in 1848, and John C. Fremont in 1856—could boast wide experience in the rugged
West, even if born to well-to-do families. No one aside from Andrew Jackson, who
was orphaned by age twelve, could claim such childhood deprivation and sorrow as
did Lincoln, but the apparent anomaly that a silk-hatted rhetorician could have sprung
from the greasy tables and coonskin couture of rural America was still then difficult
to grasp.

Yet the self-made man was an American phenomenon, and Lincoln embodied it
truly and thoroughly. He broke fresh prairie with a team of animals on that man's farm,
then turned to the same work on his own father's Illinois land, and went on to re-cast
the laws to allow any one in any state to try his hand at the same. ∞

---

*". . . the self-made man was an American phenomenon, and Lincoln
embodied it truly and thoroughly."*

Springfield, Ills. Aug. 24. 1860

John Hanks, Esq
My dear Sir:
Yours of the 23rd is received— My recollection is that I never lived in the same neighborhood with Charles Hanks till I came to Macon county, Illinois, after I was twenty one years of age— As I understand, he and I were born in different counties of Kentucky, and never saw each other in that State; that while I was a very small boy my father removed to Indiana, and your father with his family remained in Kentucky for many years— At length you, a young man grown, came to our neighborhood, and were at our house, off and on, a great deal for three, four, a five years; and during the time, your father, with his whole family, except William, Charles, and William Miller, who had married one of your sisters, came to the same neighborhood in Indiana, and remained a year or two, and then went to Illinois— William, Charles, and William Miller, had removed directly from Kentucky to Illinois, not even passing through our neighborhood in Indiana. Once, a year or two before I came to Illinois, Charles, with some other, had been back to Kentucky, and returning to Illinois, passed through our neighborhood in Indiana. He stopped, I think, but one day, (certainly not so much as three); and this was the first time I ever saw him in my life, and the only time, till I came to Illinois, as before stated. The year I passed in Macon county I was with him a good deal— mostly on his own place, where I helped him at breaking prairie, with a joint team of his and ours which, in turn, broke some on the new place we were improving—

This is, as I remember it— Dont let this letter be made public by any means—

Yours very truly
A Lincoln

47

"Under the Veil"

The "Black" Republican

1860/1864

LEO TOLSTOY ONCE SAID THAT "THE GREATNESS OF NAPOLEON, CAE-
sar, and Washington is only moonlight by the sun of Lincoln." Walt Whitman deemed
him "the grandest figure on the crowded canvas of the drama of the nineteenth century," and historians generally rank him as one of the three greatest presidents of all
time, if not the greatest. So it is difficult to imagine, let alone believe, that Lincoln was
ever thought incompetent and ineffective, despised or hated. But he most certainly
was. In this context and in light of the racist views of many across the land in the mid-
nineteenth century, it is no surprise that he was labeled "Abraham Africanus the First"
and that effigy dolls were created to protest Lincoln and his antislavery views, whether
he advocated stopping slavery's spread or abolishing it altogether.

A mid-nineteenth-century folk art effigy doll is a rather unsettling and very rare
artifact in the ALPLM's collection. Most effigy dolls were thrown into bonfires at
anti-Republican rallies. This one depicts Lincoln dressed in a long black frock coat, bow
tie, buttoned shirt, weskit, with gray trousers. The effigy's creator enhanced Lincoln's
face by using pencil and watercolor on an onionskin or tracing-paper mask, topping
the doll with real hair, which is used to tie the mask to the head. At first glance, the
depiction of Lincoln is fairly representative, but as the paper mask is lifted, it reveals
Lincoln in black face. The doll's depiction is similar to an 1862 engraving called "Under
the Veil" by Adalbert Volck, which also depicts Lincoln, once unveiled, as a black man.

Lincoln, a champion of the black race, was known by his adversaries as a "black
Republican" because he helped establish and was a member of the Republican Party—
the antislavery party. Detractors like Bavarian-born, Confederate sympathizer Volck
and the creator of the effigy doll showed their distaste for Lincoln and his policies
through creative artistic expression. Effigy dolls, political cartoons, or engravings had
no effect on Lincoln. As a man of steady countenance, he was not swayed by what
others thought of him and approached the issue of slavery and its abolition with unde-
terred, single-minded focus. Both his Emancipation Proclamation and the Thirteenth
Amendment he strongly endorsed successfully came to pass, leaving the so-called reign
of "Abraham Africanus the First" a triumphant success, albeit one wherein the protag-
onist meets a tragic ending. ⌘

The depiction of Lincoln (left) is fairly representative, but as the mask is lifted (right), it reveals Lincoln in black face.

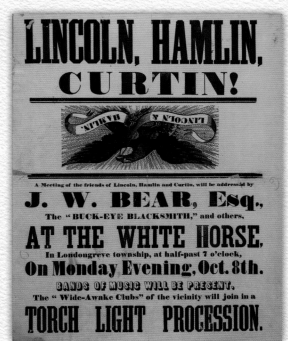

Lincoln and Hamlin

The Campaign of 1860

1860

48

SINCE THE 1960s, TELEVISION HAS LED TO MORE OF AN EMPHASIS ON the colors of political elections. So has the color-coding of the two main parties as Democratic-blue and Republican-red (which, before the 1990s, was the other way around). In 1860 there was much more color in the printing and dyeing of campaign materials than in years past, and the clearest choice in a generation of which party was "right" and which was "wrong" (depending on one's opinion).

The manufacturing of flags like the one shown here from Lincoln's 1860 presidential campaign was nearly always devised at the home or very local level. So too were the pins, ribbons, the political tickets—what the voter actually carried with him to the polling place—and even the largest banners. The nation barely had "national" party organizations, just as both sides relied on state-level militia during the first part of the war and continued to rely almost entirely on state-level recruitment of new regiments thereafter. Campaign organization fell to local news editors, photographers, ribbon-makers, engravers, and broadside printers. The Republicans happened to have held a clear majority of support among skilled printing tradesmen that year and in 1864, so that new and innovative announcements for Lincoln and Hamlin, or Lincoln and Johnson in 1864, held the visual field.

The flag shown here is not pristine. Cotton, linen, wool, and silk are all frangible threads, especially when they are folded repeatedly, and this example was kept flat over the years but wrapped with its wooden pole, leaching acidic tannin onto the fabric. ◯

49 Lincoln, the Candidate

Building a Bridge

1864

In 1864 as the tide of the war was turning and thoughts and plans for Reconstruction were becoming more and more prevalent, Lincoln ran for a second term against his former major general, Democrat George B. McClellan. Lincoln ran on the Union ticket, looking to the future—a future without his current vice president, Hannibal Hamlin. Although Hamlin of Maine proved a competent leader in the US Senate and sound antislavery running mate, Lincoln was not assured a clear path to victory in 1864 and felt that selection of a southerner committed to unity was key.

The wartime military governor of Tennessee, Andrew Johnson, a Lincoln appointee, was thought to be the ideal candidate for vice president. He had been the only senator who did not leave Congress when his home state seceded, because he was a southerner committed to the Union. He thereby provided a bridge between the North and South as the nation looked forward to postwar Reconstruction. The Lincoln-Johnson campaign flag of 1864, like the flags from the Campaign of 1860, is made of linen in the image of the American flag. This flag depicts thirty-six five-pointed stars (there had been thirty-three states during the 1860 campaign, and Nevada made thirty-six in October 1864). The stars on homemade flags did not always match the number of states, because it was more important to get the name of the candidates in front of the public than it was to create an exact historical representation. The Lincoln-Johnson flag, like those used in the Campaign of 1860, was carried by supporters at rallies, parades, and marches, much like those sponsored by the Wide Awakes during Lincoln's first presidential bid. The colorful campaign flag is a reminder of Lincoln the candidate, and of how nineteenth-century political campaigns were just as spirited, expressive, and supportive as those in the twentieth and twenty-first centuries.

The original owners of this flag would have been pleased that their candidates won the election and were sworn into office on March 4, 1865. Yet in just over a month, Lincoln would be assassinated, and Andrew Johnson would be sworn in as the seventeenth president of the United States. In the end, the selection of Johnson as his vice president would prove to be one of Abraham Lincoln's less successful decisions, as history has shown Johnson to be more providential than presidential—a lackluster "leader" who was thrust into the presidency on the strength of an assassin's bullet. ∞

Andrew Johnson is the Andrew Jackson
of the war . . . I have the greatest confidence
in him. —ABRAHAM LINCOLN

"Abraham Lincoln, Union Forever"

A Soldier Campaigns for Lincoln

JULY 22, 1864

LIEUTENANT JOHN PHILIPS OF THE 6TH REGIMENT OF KANSAS Cavalry wrote from camp near Fort Smith, Arkansas, in the summer of 1864 to his friend David McCormick in Schuyler County, Illinois. Philips evidently had formerly lived in Schuyler County, as he knew many of the people still there during the war and was curious about their political tendencies now. He also predicted that McCormick would soon find a girl to marry. Angry that Copperheads (pro-rebel Democrats) seemed to be numerous in Schuyler, he reported that nearly all of the soldiers in his unit favored Lincoln's re-election that fall; that he could not comprehend the lack of patriotism of those who did not support Lincoln and the war effort against slavery; and that the new black troops in the midst of the 6th Kansas made the best guards, for they knew the local terrain and were vigilant against the enemy.

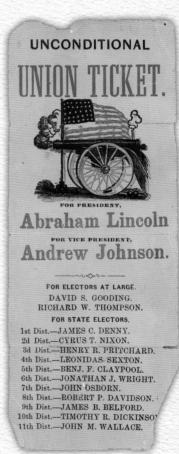

Philips also wrote of prices: "Here in this forsaken country every thing is very high at Ft Smith. Flour is selling at thirty dollars per barrel. Coffee one dollar per pound. Potatoes three dollars per bushel. Butter fifty cents per pound. . . . it is the fruits of secession." As a representative soldier letter, however, it possesses one very unusual feature: He used the final side of his letter as a makeshift campaign poster that read, Abraham Lincoln, Union Forever, perhaps hoping that McCormick would post it somewhere noticeable as the election season began. ☙

6th Regiment, Kansas cavalry lieutenant John Philips campaigns
for the president with his pen, "Abraham Lincoln, Union Forever."

51 Quiet Ambition

Lincoln Assesses the Numbers

December 1, 1864

AMBITION IS EXPECTED BUT SOMETIMES GOES UNRECOGNIZED IN politicians. On two long sheets of paper in the days and weeks after his re-election on November 8, 1864, Lincoln wrote out the votes for and against his national candidacies, giving us a window for peering in as he crafts and assesses policy. The left column, 1860, is all in ink, since those 1860 totals were official. The votes in the right column, some in ink and others in pencil, were still coming in from each state. Which states felt a growing satisfaction with the Republican's administration? In which was it declining? Thus, we can see he had gained relative support in Illinois and Massachusetts, but lost some in New York and Connecticut. Through the logic of the Electoral College, never have New Hampshire's or California's five electoral votes looked as big as they did in 1864. Yet these were all small movements within the majorities won by Lincoln and Andrew Johnson in nearly all northern states.

Lincoln compiled these figures in part to recite in his annual message to Congress on December 6. He told of the total number of votes *cast* in the states to underscore the very fact that regular elections were being held again in all northern states, the four border states, and the new states of Kansas, West Virginia, and Nevada. Indeed, for the first time *in recorded history* open elections were held during a civil war. Furthermore, the growing vote *total* since 1860 answered his critics: "that we have *more* men *now* than we had when the war *began*; that we are not exhausted, nor in process of exhaustion; that we are *gaining* strength. . . ." Lincoln commented on strong immigration to the North. Unsaid was the common knowledge that the rebels were nearly out of men.

Lincoln also mentally calculated from these columns which states might or might not ratify a Thirteenth Amendment if and when it got through Congress. Some of his hopes and plans for Reconstruction are thus found silently between these columns. Not all politics are local: columns of figures, like columns of men, can ventriloquize for national purposes, and for all mankind. ∽

	1860	1864	
California	118.840	110.000	
Connecticut	77.246	86.616	
Delaware	16.039	16.924	
Illinois	339.693	348.235	
Indiana	272.143	280.645	
Iowa	128.331	143.331	
Kentucky	146.216	90.000	
Maine	97.918	111.000	
Maryland	92.502	72.703	
Massachusetts	169.533	175.487	
Michigan	154.747	162.413	
Minnesota	34.799	42.500	
Missouri	165.538	90.000	
New Hampshire	65.953	69.111	
New Jersey	121.125	128.680	
New York	675.156	730.664	
Ohio	442.441	470.558	487.102
Oregon	14.410	14.410	
Pennsylvania	476.442	571.000	
Rhode Island	19.931	22.187	
Vermont	42.844	55.811	
West Virginia	46.195	33.874	
Wisconsin	152.180	146.000	
	3.870.222	3.958.693	
		3.870.222	

	Increase	88.471	
Add Kansas		23.000	really, 17.234 Soldiers not noted
" Nevada		16.528	16.528
		127.999	33.762
			3582.011
Soldiers voted more than		16.500	4015.773
" R.J.		3.000	3.870.222
" N.J.		7.500	145.551
" Del.		1.500	
" Ia.		16.500	
" Ills.		21.500	
		193.999	
Cal.		4.500	

52

The Shaken, Shaking Hand

The Right Hand of Lincoln

1869

LEONARD VOLK HOLDS AN UNUSUAL CONNECTION TO ABRAHAM Lincoln. He was born in 1828 to farmwork in an Adirondack village in New York, and by 1857 made his way to the booming frontier city of Chicago. There he dominated the sculpting field, small though it was, in part because he had the good fortune to have married a cousin of Stephen A. Douglas. Volk was, like most artists then and now, a Democrat. His wealthy, politically influential relative had sent him to Italy for two years to study classical art before he might conquer Chicago. Volk put his native skills and high training to the service of making *inter alia*, a life mask of his patron Senator Douglas, and later made the standing figure atop the column at Douglas's Tomb in Chicago.

Next came a mask of Abraham Lincoln. Volk presciently did this in plaster, in Chicago in March 1860, *before* the Republican Party's nomination, and the hands of Lincoln in June in Springfield, two weeks *after* the nomination. An oft-told tale is how Lincoln's right hand was so swollen from greeting his well-wishers that day, that the sculptor had to saw off a broom handle for the candidate to grasp, lest his sore twitching muscles shake off the wet plaster.

Upon Volk's return to Rome in 1869, he made Lincoln "classical" by creating the polished white marble hand shown here, based on the earlier plaster hand. There is no other known example in marble of this sculpture. It has appeared at major exhibitions in Chicago, Los Angeles, and Springfield. In the 1990s a Volk descendant allowed the sculptor's scrapbooks about his growing renown, his thinking, and his methods to be broken up and sold piecemeal, so we may never know exactly when the various other reproductions of Lincoln masks and hands were made, by him or by others.

It's strange that Lincoln, a rough-hewn orator-woodsman, is enshrined in marble like an ancient imperial emperor. And how strange that the agent of that transformation, four years after the Emancipator's death, was a man from a small snowbound town who prospered in the roughest windy city. Also uncanny: Volk named his son Douglas, in honor of his Democratic patron. Douglas Volk became a painter, who used his father's sculptures to model a series of oil portraits of the great Republican. One hangs in the White House, which was built in an ancient architectural style, just as its nation was giving birth to modern democratic geniuses from nowhere. ∽

Abraham Lincoln entering Richmond (top) and delivering his Second Inaugural Address (bottom)

PART 5
President and Commander-in-Chief

A. Lincoln

Lincoln's presidential wax seal

53

The Face of the Presidency

The Man behind the Masks

1860 AND 1865

IT IS OFTEN SAID THAT THE OFFICE OF PRESIDENT OF THE UNITED States ages a person. The American presidency is demanding, thankless, and fraught with stressful challenges, debates, and crises. Perhaps no other president in the history of the United States had a more challenging and stressful tenure than Abraham Lincoln.

Shortly after his election, South Carolina seceded from the Union, followed by the start of the American Civil War just forty days into his presidency. Ten more states seceded over the next six months. In addition to the issues and concerns faced by all presidents, Abraham Lincoln had to deal with the possible implosion of the United States. With the "more perfect Union" not only growing less perfect and less united, the grand American experiment in democracy threatened to become a colossal, dismal failure.

One need only look at the two life masks cast from Abraham Lincoln's face to see the tremendous toll the war, the slavery question, and the presidency as a whole took on him. The two masks in the ALPLM's collection represent the only two ever cast of his face. The first was cast in Chicago in 1860 while Lincoln was campaigning for the Republican nomination for the presidency. Lincoln was fifty-one years old. The Italian-trained sculptor was the American Leonard W. Volk. Volk's mask shows a whisker-free Lincoln with a vigorous and rugged countenance.

The second mask was made in Washington, DC, in 1865 by Clark Mills, another American sculptor, who was able to cast Lincoln's face about two months prior to his assassination. Mills's mask shows a bearded Lincoln, age fifty-six, who has aged considerably. His face is drawn, his expression languid and melancholic. While photographs exist that also reveal the quickly aging president in the same span of years, no photographs are more revealing in their dimensionality than the two sculptures of Lincoln's face.

Lincoln, who was not fond of the casting process, sat patiently for both Volk and Mills. He also had casts of his hands made by Volk shortly after he had won his party's nomination for the presidency. Copies of those casts are in the ALPLM's collection as well. The Volk and Mills casts leave exact impressions of the sixteenth president and evidence of the uncompromising, relentless, and unforgiving nature of the presidency itself. ∽

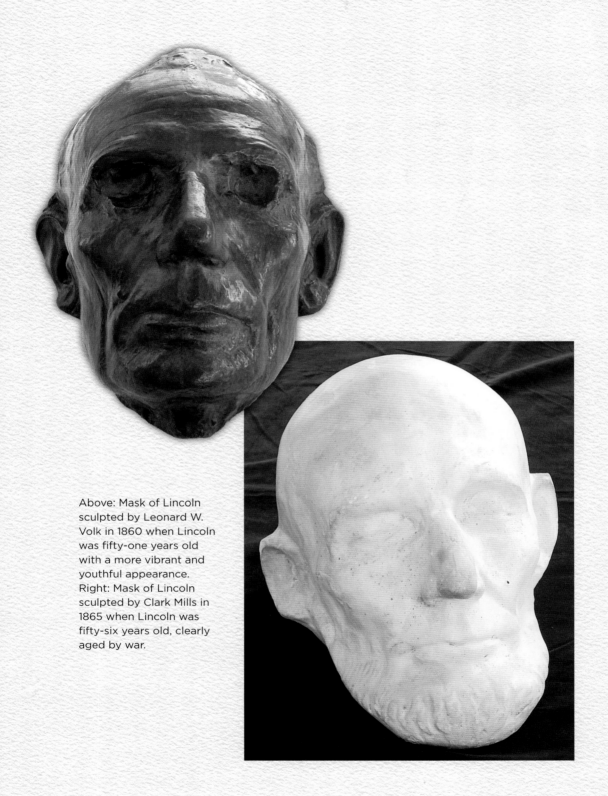

Above: Mask of Lincoln sculpted by Leonard W. Volk in 1860 when Lincoln was fifty-one years old with a more vibrant and youthful appearance.
Right: Mask of Lincoln sculpted by Clark Mills in 1865 when Lincoln was fifty-six years old, clearly aged by war.

A Historic Memento

Abraham Lincoln's Briefcase

1861

54

AS IS OFTEN THE CASE ON SPECIAL PRESIDENTIAL OCCASIONS, MEMENTOS are given in remembrance of a historic event. In the later twentieth and early twenty-first centuries, presidents often gave pens used to sign special legislation into law to people instrumental in helping the laws come to pass. On March 4, 1861, Lincoln and each member of his Cabinet were given a briefcase. Abraham Lincoln's, of course, is distinguished by his name stamped with gilt letters.

Might the briefcase have contained the original draft of the Emancipation Proclamation on which he began working in the summer of 1862? After all, this was the briefcase many believe Lincoln carried during his frequent three-mile trips from the White House to the Soldiers' Home—Mr. Lincoln's nineteenth-century version of Camp David. And it was at the Soldiers' Home where Abraham Lincoln wrote the beginnings of the Proclamation, sitting at a desk from which he could hear and sometimes see Union troops returning from the front carrying their dead and dying. Or might the briefcase have been used in 1863 to carry some initial thoughts for the Gettysburg Address, or in 1865 to carry scribbled notes as he prepared to write his Second Inaugural Address? All of these are possibilities, but one thing is certain: The distressed brown-leather case is well worn and was well used by its owner. Folding back the curved flap, one can see on its underside a few bits of red sealing wax, no doubt from confidential correspondence or important documents bearing his presidential seal.

After his father's death, Robert Todd Lincoln kept the case, which eventually came into the possession of the Heyser family, who long worked for the president's eldest son. What is most striking about the case is Abraham Lincoln's name. It is embossed in gold capital letters in the center bottom of its flap and is punctuated by a period. It is as though the manufacturer (a government contractor, now unknown), understood the future immortality of the man and that the name ABRAHAM LINCOLN was enough. Period. Full stop. No explanations necessary. ∽

55 From Sea to Shining Sea

Lincoln Builds a Railroad

1853

It is difficult to imagine a time when the American railroad did not extend from sea to shining sea. The vision for a transcontinental railroad did not begin with Abraham Lincoln, but it ended, or more to the point, was *fulfilled* because of him. Like most concerns in mid-nineteenth-century America, the western expansion of the railroad centered on the slavery question. Elected to the presidency in 1852, Franklin Pierce was anxious to keep the peace in a nation becoming more and more divided by the opposing views of the Whigs and Democrats in terms of expansion, containment, or the end of slavery and involuntary servitude.

There is no better example of these opposing views than the building of the American transcontinental railroad. Most Whigs desired a northern route for the railroad, most Democrats, a southern one. Expansion of the railroad meant broadening the western frontier, strengthening the southern and northern economies, and with it, the Democrats hoped, slavery's expansion. In 1853, President Pierce, a Democrat, ordered his secretary of war Jefferson Davis to have a scientific study conducted hoping it would support the theory that a southern route for the railroad was optimal, as the most expedient route to transport cotton to the Pacific shores, and from there to East Asia. The results of the study were bound into the thirteen-volume *Reports of Explorations and Surveys . . .* which is better known today as the *Transcontinental Railroad Report*. A folio-size, leather-bound copy of the report came into the possession of Abraham Lincoln in 1860. Lincoln likely read parts of the scientific analyses but perhaps mainly the political or policy summaries in order to clearly understand the issue at hand.

In 1862, he signed into law the Pacific Railway Act, which set a northern course for the railroad from Chicago to Omaha and then on to San Francisco to expedite the transportation of lumber, grain, and other northern goods to California and then perhaps East Asia. Sadly, Lincoln did not live to see the railroads linked. On May 10, 1869, the "Golden Spike"—the last spike needed to connect the Union Pacific and the Central Pacific railroads—was ceremonially hammered in at Promontory Summit in the Utah Territory. The *Transcontinental Railroad Report* remained in President Lincoln's possession until his death, when the volumes passed on to his heirs. ☙

33d Congress, }
2d Session. }

HOUSE OF REPRESENTATIVES.

{ Ex. Doc.
{ No. 91.

REPORTS

OF

EXPLORATIONS AND SURVEYS,

TO

ASCERTAIN THE MOST PRACTICABLE AND ECONOMICAL ROUTE FOR A RAILROAD

FROM THE

MISSISSIPPI RIVER TO THE PACIFIC OCEAN.

MADE UNDER THE DIRECTION OF THE SECRETARY OF WAR, IN

1853-4,

ACCORDING TO ACTS OF CONGRESS OF MARCH 3, 1853, MAY 31, 1854, AND AUGUST 5, 1854.

VOLUME I.

WASHINGTON:
A. O. P. NICHOLSON, PRINTER.
1855.

56

"Out of Many, One"

The Presidential Dinner Service

1861

WHEN ABRAHAM LINCOLN WAS GROWING UP IN A DIRT-FLOOR CABIN in Kentucky, the family meals were most likely served on wood or clay pottery. Conversely, Abraham's bride-to-be, Mary Todd, grew up in a privileged household in Lexington, Kentucky. Her father, Robert Todd, a wealthy businessman and banker, saw to it that Mary received the finest life had to offer. She was well educated and attended finishing school. She was attuned to the social graces befitting those of high society, which included dining on the Todd family's white and green painted porcelain china.

Given Abraham and Mary's divergent backgrounds, it was clearly Mary's influence and refined taste that was reflected in the two sets of White House china produced during the Lincoln presidency. One pattern was the official service of the Lincoln presidency; the other was the family's private service (see pages 28–29).

When the Lincolns first arrived at the White House in 1861, they found mostly mix-and-match china, but no complete set. Feeling it would be important to uphold the dignity of the presidency, they asked for and received an appropriation from Congress to purchase a formal service. The set Mary purchased is Haviland, from Limoges, France, then considered the best and most popular china in the 1860s. The service was designed and manufactured in France and "finished" with colors in New York, in 1861. Interestingly, there is no maker's mark on the pieces, as Haviland did not begin using one until about a decade later.

The ALPLM has both a dinner and a dessert plate as part of its collection. Made for official use at state dinners, the center of each plate is decorated with a variation of the Great Seal designed by Charles Thomson and adopted by Congress in 1782 that depicts, as Thomson wrote, "an American eagle on the wing and rising." The eagle holds in his right talon an olive branch representing the power of peace and in his left talon thirteen arrows representing the power of war. A shield is placed below the eagle bearing a constellation of stars and thirteen stripes. A ribbon with the American motto, *E Pluribus Unum*—"Out of Many, One"—flies beneath the eagle, underscoring the Lincolns' singular goal of preserving the Union. It is encircled by a solferino (purple-red) colored band with gold designs. The service is priceless, as one also considers the events at which and by whom it was used. Future American presidents such as Benjamin Harrison and John F. Kennedy chose to honor Lincoln by replicating the pattern during their respective presidencies. ∽

57

War's Grisly Reminder

The Surgical Kit

1861–1865

LINCOLN WAS CONFRONTED ALMOST DAILY WITH THE EFFECTS OF HIS wartime decisions. This was especially so as he spent more and more time at "The Cottage," his refuge and safe haven from the politics and pressures of Washington, DC, and the constant barrage of visitors to the White House. The Cottage was on the northern outskirts of the city on the site of the Old Soldiers' Home. It afforded Lincoln the sad opportunity to be even nearer to the brave soldiers returning from the front, many of whom would die at nearby hospitals. For Lincoln, there was no escaping the grim realities of the war. When he spoke at Gettysburg, the bodies of many of the fallen awaiting burial lay in close proximity to the platform on which he stood.

After the fall of Richmond, he again saw firsthand the ugly effects of war as he crossed the still-smoking battlefields. As though the threat of being shot or blown apart by cannon fire was not enough, the Civil War soldier also faced the danger of going under the surgeon's knife. Out in the battlefield, a tent or an abandoned building could become a makeshift hospital wherein the surgeon would employ the implements from his surgical kit in an attempt, often futile, to save a steady stream of victims. Many soldiers survived the surgery only to fall victim to infection.

Viewing the Civil War surgical kit in the ALPLM's collection is an encounter with mid-nineteenth-century wartime surgical practices. The wooded box reveals, among other things, a steel bone saw, a small axe, clamps, knives, scalpels, and probes of varying sizes, not unlike the ones used to remove the assassin's bullet from Lincoln's brain the night he was shot at Ford's Theatre.

Because of Lincoln's proximity to the front, it is not too far afield to suggest that he had occasion to see such a kit as it was used on the gallant soldiers who survived not just the war, but field surgery. The kit is a grisly reminder of the brutality of war, whether in the taking or saving of a life. ☾

". . . that, from these honored dead we take increased devotion to that cause for which they here, gave the last full measure of devotion . . ."

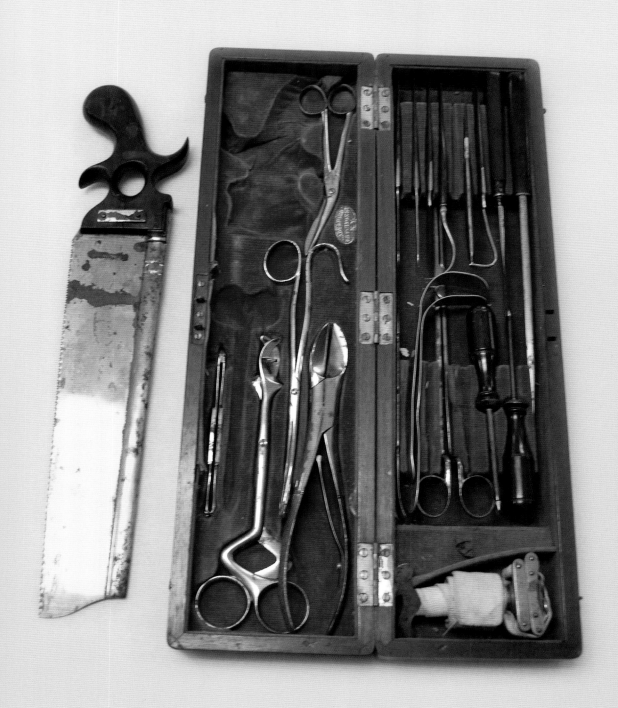

58 Hierarchy Trumps Democracy

The Attorney General's Opinion

MARCH 15, 1861

AS SCRUPULOUS AN ATTORNEY AS LINCOLN WAS, HE DID QUICKLY SET his foot down about hierarchy within his Cabinet, and made it clear that he would be its leader even though the party's senior figure William H. Seward expected to be something like a prime minister to the underprepared prairie attorney. Yet Lincoln's deference to his colleagues took important form at crucial moments, such as the decision about when to issue the Emancipation Proclamation, and about when, if at all, to replace General McClellan as his leading field commander.

The first and perhaps key time when he sought the counsel of all wise heads came on March 15, 1861, over the watershed issue of defending federal property against rebels. Lincoln solicited each Cabinet member's opinion in writing, first, about the wisdom of re-provisioning the forts with food and medicine only. Here is the letter to Attorney General Edward Bates, the oldest member of the seven-man parliament-in-miniature.

Five of the seven were against the idea, fearing that it would provoke shooting. Bates was among those five, basing his judgment on "prudence and patriotism only," not on the "question of lawful right, nor physical power." The two colleagues who saw wisdom in the effort to re-provision—that is, to assert an initial level of firm support for a right to come and go from federal properties—were the Cabinet's most liberal and its most conservative members: Salmon P. Chase and Montgomery Blair. The latter, from a formerly slave-holding Maryland family, backed "measures which will inspire respect for the power of the Government." Chase, for his part, did not think that the re-provisioning action would lead to war.

So it was that the three, including Lincoln, prevailed over the five. Hierarchy trumped democracy. As has more recently been said within the US military forces, "We defend democracy. We don't practice it internally."

Bates generally upheld Lincoln's legal views over the next three-plus years. He resigned his office right after Lincoln's re-election in November 1864, somewhat worried about the effects of the abolition movement making way in the form of the Thirteenth Amendment, but more so because at age seventy-one he missed his St. Louis home and, honestly, wanted to spend more time with his beloved wife Julia, their eight children, and their countless grandchildren. One of those surviving sons was an officer in the Confederate army. ❦

Executive Mansion
March 15. 1861
The Honorable Attorney General:
My Dear Sir:
Assuming it to be possible to now provision Fort Sumter, under all the circumstances, is it wise to attempt it?
Please give me your opinion, in writing, on this question.
Your obedient Servant
A. Lincoln

My dear Sir
    Assuming it to be possible to now provision Fort-Sumter, under all the circumstances, is it wise to attempt it?
    Please give me your opinion, in writing, on this question.
                Your Ob't Serv't, A. Lincoln

59

Sarcasm and Strategy

Lincoln Removes Little Napoleon

OCTOBER 24, 1862

GEORGE B. MCCLELLAN WAS THE SON OF A WEALTHY PHILADELPHIA doctor. At West Point he finished second in his class, and served in the Mexican-American War. At the outbreak of the Civil War, McClellan—unlike a majority of his West Point brethren—remained loyal to the North, though he was pro-slavery.

He led successful attacks on small rebel units and was hailed as "Little Napoleon" or "Little Mac" because of his short stature. President Lincoln was obliged by public pressure to place him in command of the Army of the Potomac by the end of 1861. McClellan rudely refused to serve under the aged general-in-chief Winfield Scott and was soon ignoring Lincoln's orders as well.

Lincoln ordered him to make a full frontal advance on enemy lines in Virginia on Washington's Birthday in 1862, but McClellan failed to try that. He was always requesting more men, horses, and supplies. He did not wish to bruise his illustrious army, harm old classmates in the other camp, or see slavery end. Only by luck—a corporal had found some rebel battle plans in a field—did McClellan turn back Lee at Antietam on September 17, 1862. And when Lincoln urged McClellan to pursue and capture the wounded rebel army, Little Mac declined. His army was tired, he telegraphed to Washington, and needed rest.

Thus, on October 24, 1862, Lincoln wrote his sarcastic reply to McClellan's latest complaint.

Upon receipt the general made further excuses. Lincoln partly apologized for his temper and asked him to move. Nothing happened.

Why had not Lincoln demoted the general for insubordination? Because McClellan was by some measure the most prominent Democrat in the Union army. Lincoln could not remove such a man before the midterm elections. So he waited, and Lee returned safely to Virginia, ready to defeat Union general Ambrose Burnside at Fredericksburg, Virginia, on December 13.

On the day after the midterm elections, Lincoln removed McClellan from command. The Republicans lost about thirty-five seats in Congress that week, partly due to the still tentative Emancipation Proclamation and partly because of military humiliations. Or, because of horses with sore tongues. ∽

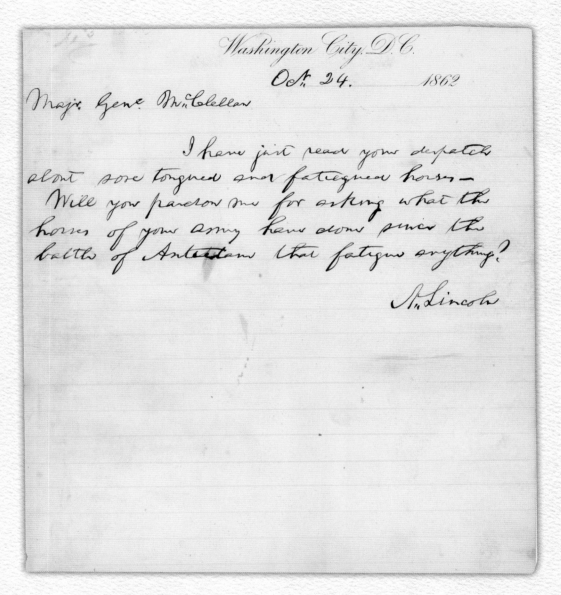

Majr. Genl. McClellan
    I have just read your despatch about sore tongued and fatiegued horses. Will you pardon me for asking what the horses of your army have done since the battle of Antietam that fatigue anything?

                                                A. Lincoln

Three Medals of Honor bestowed for "gallantry in action" during the American Civil War: Andrew Jackson Smith's Medal (upper left), John Warden's Medal (upper right), and Loyd Wheaton's Medal (bottom center)

Gallantry in Action

Medals of Honor

1862–1865

60

MOST PEOPLE, WERE THEY TO WALK IN THE SIXTEENTH PRESIDENT'S shoes, would find the Civil War and the abolishment of slavery enough to focus on during a presidency. But Abraham Lincoln was the ultimate multitasker, who set his sights on a broader vision for America. In 1862 alone, he signed into law the Homestead Act, which deeded land to pioneers settling America's western frontier; the Pacific Railway Act, which paved the way for a transcontinental railroad; and the Morrill Land Grant Act, which established land grant universities in each state. In addition, Lincoln established the US Department of Agriculture to advance America's agrarian society, and the National Academy of Sciences. He also quietly and purposefully created the Medal of Honor that recognizes the gallantry of members of the Armed Services.

The Medal of Honor is our nation's highest honor, given to "officers and privates as shall most distinguish themselves by their gallantry in action, and other soldier-like qualities." Lincoln, who once said, "Honor to the Soldier and Sailor everywhere, who bravely bears his country's cause," often spent his days visiting wounded men in hospitals or camps. He understood their bravery and gallantry both on and off the field of battle. He understood that recognition of their valor was needed.

The ALPLM has in its collection three Medals of Honor. The first was bestowed upon John Warden "for gallantry in the charge of the volunteer storming party . . ." at Vicksburg, Mississippi, in May 1863. The second was bestowed upon Loyd Wheaton for being "first to enter the enemy's works, against a strong fire of artillery and infantry" at Fort Blakeley, Alabama, in April 1865. The third was bestowed upon Andrew Jackson Smith for "saving his regimental colors, after the color bearer was killed during a bloody charge called the Battle of Honey Hill, South Carolina" in November 1864.

The original medals, made of bronze, consist of an inverted five-point star with laurel and oak leaves symbolizing victory and strength, respectively, and thirty-four stars based on the number of stars on the American flag in 1862. Each medal bears the ribbon used at the time at which it was *issued*, rather than when it was *earned*—just one of the ways in which he could "bind up the nation's wounds," and "care for him who shall have borne the battle." ∞

61 The New York Draft Riots

Lincoln Holds His Ground

AUGUST 10, 1863

FIVE CITIES SAW RIOTING IN THE HOT SUMMER OF 1863. BY FAR THE worst episodes engulfed lower Manhattan in mid-July, following the president's order to begin a military draft. This was the most serious northern challenge to authority during Lincoln's term. Yet four weeks later he ordered that the draft go ahead, assigning 2,050 men of that portion of the city toward the national effort. On August 10 his signature indicated that despite congressional, press, and public opposition, Lincoln would press ahead.

In the same week he wrote to Governor Horatio Seymour, a Democrat, to repel his charges that New York was already putting forth more than its fair percentage of men to the Union effort. As Lincoln held, "the drawing will be made upon the quotas as now fixed." About 150 fewer men were demanded by the order here than was sketched out in the original calculations, likely as a way to mollify Seymour and others who called the draft "unconstitutional."

Who had rioted? Mostly Irish laborers, nearly all of them voters or potential voters for the Democrats, and nearly all of them violently opposed to black equality or even presence in an army or labor force. Fiery attacks on the offices of Republican newspapers might have been inspired by political motives, but the intentional burning of a Negro orphanage was not. An estimated three hundred people were killed in the riots, which lasted three or four days, and were quelled mainly by the arrival of additional Union troops from the field, some of them having fought at Gettysburg a month earlier and still bandaged or tired or both.

As the war progressed and along with it the work toward blacks' rights, many leaders of the opposition to Lincoln continued to hail from New York City. Brothers Fernando and Benjamin Wood, both in Congress at one time and Fernando a one-time mayor of New York, led calls against a Thirteenth Amendment. Their side lost, even as their political party lost, even as their nation prevailed in the war. Deaths of New York volunteers were indeed slightly higher than a strict percentage of their numbers in the armed forces might predict, mainly because so many upstaters volunteered early on, and New Yorkers were so prominent in the Eastern Theater late in the war when General Grant hammered away at rebel defenses in Virginia. The three hundred civilian deaths in July 1863, however, were unaccountably disproportionate to the grievance of the antiwar faction. ⌀

EXECUTIVE MANSION,

Washington, D. C., Aug. 10th, 1863.

I, ABRAHAM LINCOLN, President of the United States of America, and Commander=in=chief of the Army and Navy thereof, having taken into consid= eration the number of volunteers and militia furnished by and from the several States, including the State of *New York*, and the period of service of said volunteers and militia since the commencement of the present rebellion, in order to equalize the numbers among the Districts of the said States, and having considered and allowed for the number already furnished as aforesaid, and the time of their service aforesaid, do hereby assign *Two Thousand and Fifty (2050)* as the first proportional part of the quota of troops to be furnished by the *2nd* DISTRICT OF THE STATE OF *New York* under this, the first call made by me on the State of *New York*, under the act approved March 3, 1863, entitled "An Act for Enrolling and Calling out the National Forces, and for other purposes," and, in pursuance of the act aforesaid, I order that a draft be made in the said *2nd* DISTRICT OF THE STATE OF *New York* for the number of men herein assigned to said District, and FIFTY PER CENT. IN ADDITION.

IN WITNESS WHEREOF, I have hereunto set my hand and caused the seal of the United States to be affixed.

Done at the City of Washington, this *tenth* day of *August*, in the year of our Lord one thousand eight hundred and sixty-three, and of the independence of the United States, the eighty-eighth.

Abraham Lincoln

The Storms of Heaven and Battle

"Honor to the Soldier and Sailor"

LINCOLN WAS INVITED TO NEW YORK IN DECEMBER 1863 TO HELP THE mayor and others with volunteer recruitment, and to praise recent victories in the East. Instead, not wanting to overlook the contribution of any man in the military services, Lincoln dictated this letter to secretary John Hay, then signed it. Here is the conclusion:

> Honor to the Soldier and Sailor everywhere, who bravely bears his country's cause. Honor also to the citizen who cares for his brother in the field, and serves as he best can, the same cause. Honor to him—only less than to him who braves for the common good, the storms of heaven and the storms of battle.
>
> > Your Ob't Serv't
> > A. Lincoln

Lincoln's personal experience of military service was very limited. It entailed three months in 1832 of volunteer marching, camping, and doing battle with mosquitoes during the Black Hawk War in Illinois and Wisconsin. When he was elected captain by his mates in New Salem, he recalled in 1860 that he had "not since had any success in life" that gave him "so much satisfaction." But marching is not fighting, so he was always very quick to acknowledge and if possible reward the fighting man.

In the 1848 presidential campaign Lincoln scolded the Democratic contender, Lewis Cass, for boasting of his military successes a generation earlier, when Lincoln knew that Cass had not seen anything like the danger that most of the men had. And in his Second Inaugural Address, in 1865, Lincoln continued on this theme: "The progress of our arms, upon which all else chiefly depends."

The man that we cherish and uphold as the preserver of the Union and the abolisher of slavery would quickly have pointed to the 2.2 million men, most of them volunteers who braved "for the common good, the storms of heaven and the storms of battle." ༶

soldiers fighting elsewhere, it would be exceedingly agreeable to me to join in a suitable acknowledgement to those of the Great West, with whom I was born, and have passed my life. And it is exceedingly gratifying that a portion lately of the Army of the Potomac, but now serving with the great Army of the West, have borne so conspicuous a part in the late brilliant triumphs in Georgia.

Honor to the Soldier and Sailor everywhere, who bravely bears his country's cause. Honor also to the citizen who cares for his brother in the field, and serves as he best can, the same cause. Honor to him — only less than to him who braves, for the common good, the storms of heaven and the storms of battle.

Your Obt. Servt.
A. Lincoln

63 The Gold Hoax

Howard Strikes Again

AUGUST 22, 1864

REMEMBER THAT KERFUFFLE ABOUT LINCOLN SNEAKING THROUGH Baltimore in February 1861, disguised in Scotch plaid and cap, to avoid assassins? He did in fact take an earlier train and removed his too-visible stovepipe hat, but the Scotch plaid stuff and the scurrying about were invented by a New York reporter.

The reporter was Joseph Howard Jr., supposedly from a good Brooklyn family. Cartoonists had a field day with the imagined scene, and Lincoln opponents got lots of mileage out of it. Lincoln vowed never again to be seen "hiding" from danger.

Howard went unpunished, of course. The image was fair game: Likely he conjured it from an anecdote about how when the Scots-descended James II of Great Britain abdicated the throne, he dumped his seals of office in the Thames at the news of an invading army in the so-called "Glorious Revolution" victory for Parliament.

In May 1864 Howard struck again, but this time for money. Profiteers issued a false news report, a proclamation over Lincoln's name, that the Union's military draft would be expanded because the war was not going well. This depressed the market price of gold for two hours, allowing the fraudsters to buy it. By late morning the White House and the State Department had declared the news to be fake—a "bogus proclamation," Lincoln called it in the letter here.

Investigations revealed that at least two Democratic New York papers, and apparently one or two Republican ones, received a pre-dawn messenger with the important "news" from Washington. The Democratic papers printed it—whether conspiratorially or not is unknown. Howard and a friend (both reporters) were shown to be involved in the fakery and went to prison.

Ever the merciful one, Lincoln wrote to Secretary of War Edwin Stanton in this August 22, 1864, letter after Reverend Henry Ward Beecher of Brooklyn began to implore the president to release Howard. During his three months in prison, Howard's wife and two little daughters were suffering, according to Beecher, and he had only wanted to make "some *money*," without being aware of the political implications of the fraud. Lincoln wished to "oblige" Beecher, so both Stanton and Inspector General J. A. Hardie complied.

As Beecher concluded, Howard was "the only spotted child of a large family." ⌘

Executive Mansion,

Washington, Aug. 22, 1864.

Hon. Sec. of War

My dear Sir

I very much wish
to oblige Henry Ward Beecher,
by releasing Howard; but I
wish you to be satisfied
when it is done — What
say you?

Yours truly

A Lincoln

I have no objection if you
think it right — and this a
proper time   EMS.

Let Howard, imprisoned in regard to
the bogus proclamation, be discharged,

August 23, 1864 (over) A Lincoln

THE RED LEATHER BOX WITH GILT INLAY SHOWN HERE IS ALL THE more eye-catching because of the name on the top of its lid. The hinged box reveals a beautiful ivory-handled seal that rests on red velvet. An inscription on the inside of the lid informs us that this is the "Personal Seal of Abraham Lincoln as President of the United States of America, 1861–1865." Affixing a wax seal to an envelope or letter to keep its contents confidential was still a custom in the early- to mid-nineteenth century.

The presidential seal formally represents the office of President of the United States, which finds its roots in the seal of the president of the Continental Congress. This particular seal is one of the greatest symbols of the Lincoln presidency that now resides in the ALPLM's collection. On any given day in the White House, Abraham Lincoln would write and sign a host of letters and documents. Those he considered confidential and meant only for the designated recipient's eyes he would seal with wax. The seal's die was cast in brass. It is circular with the cut design of an American eagle with five-point stars symbolic of the thirty-six states in the Union and attached to a lathe-turned ivory handle. Nevada had just become the thirty-sixth state, eight days before Lincoln's re-election. Bits of red sealing wax are still embedded in the seal, the same type of red sealing wax found in Lincoln's briefcase. One wonders how many times he would affix this seal to important presidential communiques, and what the results may have been. No one else but Lincoln used this seal, and with it, he gave America a "new birth of freedom" and the "more perfect Union" America enjoys today. ⌒

65

In Defense of the Union

Lincoln's Greatest Weapon

1865

As a boy growing up on the frontier in a family of little means, Abraham Lincoln used a quill pen as a writing instrument rather than a nib or dip pen. Although fountain pens were widely in use by the time Lincoln reached the White House, he preferred to use quills. One of the ALPLM's prized possessions is Lincoln's white quill pen. The nine-inch-long shaft and quill point are still intact, but the feather portion is worn down. This is understandable with all the writing Lincoln had to do. It is with pens such as this that Lincoln scribbled notes or authored such great works as the Gettysburg Address, Emancipation Proclamation, or Second Inaugural Address. It is with pens such as this that Lincoln revealed his strategic brilliance, his thoughts about legislation, his practicality as well as his political acumen, and his humanity. Lincoln was a gifted writer, and the quill pen represented his weapon of choice as he proved time and again that his pen was mightier than anyone's sword. After Lincoln's death, the pen came into the possession of William H. Crook, a doorkeeper and sometime bodyguard to the president (although not on the night of the assassination). After Lincoln's death, Crook went on to serve in the administrations of all subsequent presidents up to and including Woodrow Wilson's, earning the honorary title of "colonel."

Abraham Lincoln's quill exists today as it did more than 150 years ago as a symbol of his greatest weapon in defense of the Union, in the abolition of slavery, and in the advancement of the United States of America. The knowledge and wisdom which flowed from its owner continue to advance America and the world. ∞

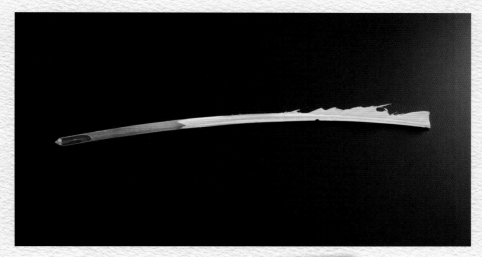

66

The "Magnificent Success"

Lincoln's Penultimate Note to Grant

APRIL 2, 1865

ABRAHAM LINCOLN AND ULYSSES S. GRANT DID NOT MEET FOR THE first time until March 8, 1864. The president had become aware of the "general who fights" in early 1862 after the breakthrough victories on the Tennessee and Cumberland Rivers far to the west, and heard regularly about him (not always to the good) after the yet-more-critical triumphs at Shiloh in April 1862 and Vicksburg in July 1863.

Some worried that Grant drank; Lincoln did not, and although there is no basis to the old joke that Lincoln said "find out what he drinks and send a case of it to each of my generals," the president did send a private investigator to Mississippi to observe Grant's behavior for a few days. Lincoln made him general-in-chief of all Union armies in March 1864 and raised him to the rank of lieutenant general—the rank held by George Washington, and since then only by Winfield Scott, who retired in 1861 after fifty-three years in the military service.

Lincoln and Grant arose from similar difficult circumstances, married well above their stations into slave-owning families, and grew morose over future prospects at points during the 1850s. They got along extremely well, entrusting to the other the duties assigned him and encroaching no further. Lincoln, after repelling many months of others' harsh comments about "Grant the Butcher" for the way he kept throwing Union men at the dwindling rebel forces, had cause for exhilaration in the note seen here.

The president came to City Point, Virginia, in late March 1865 to stay at Grant's headquarters, sensing that the end was near. Grant set out and soon reported that his men had broken through in Petersburg, Virginia, after a ten-month siege. In doing so, they effectively cut off nearly all supply to Lee's army and to the residents of Richmond. And so Lincoln wrote, on April 2, 1865, at 8:15 p.m. for the telegrapher:

"Allow me to tender to you, and all with you, the nations grateful thanks for this additional, and magnificent success. At your kind suggestion, I think I will visit you to-morrow. A. Lincoln"

This was the penultimate note Lincoln ever wrote to Grant, following up from Washington just five days later with encouragement as the general pursued Lee toward Appomattox. The note here, telling of a personal meeting on April 3, 1865—twelve months and twenty-six days after they had first met—caps off one of the briefest yet still hugely consequential relationships in world history. ∞

Head Quarters Armies of the United States,

City-Point, April. 2. 8⁴⁵ Pᵐ 865.

Lieut. General Grant.

Allow me to tender to you, and all with you, the nations grateful thanks for this additional, and magnificent success— At your kind suggestion, I think I will visit you to-morrow.

A. Lincoln

67 The Power of His Axe

An Iconic Symbol of an Iconic Man

1865

ONE OF THE EARLIEST IMAGES OF ABRAHAM LINCOLN BURNED INTO the American consciousness is that of the young "rail-splitter from Illinois" who ascended to the highest office in the land. At first glance, Lincoln hardly looked like a frontiersman, but in reality he possessed an athleticism and physicality that belied his gangly frame. The pioneer-turned-president was wiry and extraordinarily strong. Frontier work was not for the weak-willed or lazy. Although Lincoln was more cerebral than physical and preferred a good book to a hammer, spade, or plow, he could maneuver an axe like few others.

One of the artifacts in the ALPLM's collection is an axe Lincoln used exactly one week before he died. Measuring thirty two and a half inches long by seven and a half inches wide with a handle of hickory and a head of iron covered in steel, it is an iconic symbol of an iconic man. While most attention is given to Lincoln for the power of his pen, the power of his axe cannot be denied. It is a personal symbol and tool Lincoln not only used to hew rails for fences, but to hew his inner character—the strong, gritty, persevering, and courageous man Lincoln was and the leader he would become.

Lincoln used this particular axe to chop wood for the soldiers' campfire at the Depot Field Hospital, Army of the Potomac at City Point, Virginia. After a day spent shaking hands, which might ordinarily fatigue a person, Lincoln could still chop up a twenty-foot log of white oak and then perform what was known as the strongman's trick, which entailed holding his axe by the end of the handle, then extending his arm out at a ninety-degree angle to the rest of his body. The simultaneous extension of both arm and axe is extremely difficult to do, a feat of tremendous strength and ability. The axe belonged to Ulysses S. Grant's unit. It was standard Army-issue and made by the William Mann Co. in Lewistown, Pennsylvania. It is the only axe left in existence to have been authenticated as one used by the rail-splitter from Illinois. ∞

THE REAL AMERICAN
The Stuff From Which He is Made

Abraham Lincoln as "The Rail-Splitter" (1833). Painted by J. L. C. Ferris

My, how he could chop! . . . If you heard his fellin' tress in a clearin' you would say there was three men at work by the way the trees fell.—Dennis Hanks

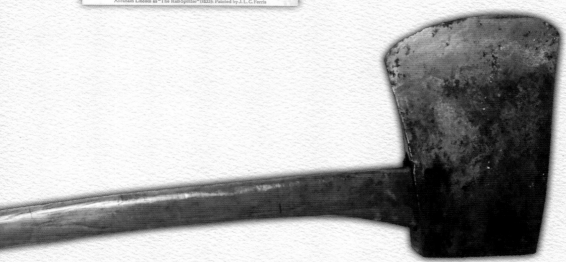

68

Holding Hands across Time

The Great Emancipator and the Bull Moose

1858–1912

HOMER DAVENPORT WAS A TALENTED CARTOONIST FOR CHICAGO newspapers around the turn of the twentieth century. He was not above some party preferences and even some specific ballyhooing for certain candidates. The upshot of a campaign speech that President Theodore Roosevelt gave in Springfield on June 3, 1904, was this original drawing. It has no caption, but its message was obvious to all who saw it—even though probably very few did actually see it—before it was inscribed to a friend, one C. J. Farrell, about two months later.

Lincoln's rise nearly split his party in 1858. A few Republicans wanted Democrat Stephen Douglas to run under both party labels. It happened again in 1860 when the eastern wing of the party was cataleptic at the unburnished and rough-shod hoss from Illinois winning the nomination in Chicago. Then in 1864 the sitting president had enough in-party challengers to his re-nomination to hold a crowded game of whist.

Theodore Roosevelt would later cause such ruckus all by himself. In 1912 he split the Republicans like a Bull Moose at a sit-down dinner, and thus handed the dessert to Democrat Woodrow Wilson. But in 1904 his re-election was simpler, even if not warmly endorsed by steady Republican Robert Lincoln, who was president of the Pullman Car Company and protector of his father's papers. Roosevelt ended up with a lock of Lincoln's hair, courtesy of his secretary of state John Hay, who acquired it in 1865, and put it into a little ring, which remained in the Roosevelt family for more than a century. Roosevelt also tried to re-launch his career with a bit of Lincoln's reputation as a re-electable Republican. In 1904 the man who carried the big stick was easily re-elected with 56 percent of the popular vote and 71 percent of the electoral vote.

So the underlying message in this drawing was obvious in 1904. Here were two Republicans holding hands, fighting the same fight against backwardness and racism. The Republican Party has been a coalition party since 1856, just as all parties must be, in a nation of hundreds of millions of people who somehow walk hand in hand still. ∞

PART 6
∽ Emancipator ∾

A. Lincoln

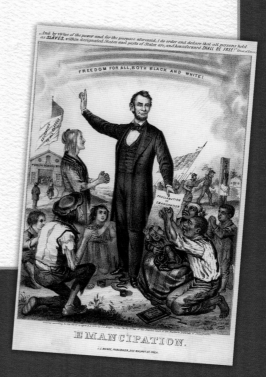

69

A Little Scrap of Paper

The Definition of Democracy

AUGUST 1, 1858

DURING THE 1858 DEBATES, LINCOLN AND DOUGLAS EACH BOILED over with ideas and words. Lincoln penned a stream of letters and speeches. Douglas spoke fluidly and angrily, tearing off his cravat when he got heated. Both men sought a US Senate seat—Douglas to retain his for a third term, and Lincoln to upset that "Little Giant."

Six books *only* about those debates have been published, and nearly every other book about Lincoln discusses that two-month period from August to October when American democracy was so wildly portrayed from differing viewpoints. Rather than addressing a wide array of political questions, they mainly addressed slavery, which is primarily why Douglas prevailed.

The little scrap of paper shown here might have boosted Lincoln into Douglas's Senate seat had it been published at the time. In all the written records of the 1858 struggle, Lincoln's words do not appear in this form. He seems literally to have kept the scrap under his hat.

"As I would not be a *slave*, so I would not be a *master*. This expresses my idea of democracy. Whatever differs from this, to the extent of the difference, is no democracy."

The note belonged to Mary Lincoln after it was found in Lincoln's office when he died. She gave it to Myra Bradwell, the first woman admitted to the bar in Illinois, who helped Mary gain her release from the insane asylum in 1875 where she had been confined for a few months because of drug addiction, hallucinations, and suicide threats.

Lincoln often stored his papers and notes in his hat while traveling. This note bears obvious marks of a tri-fold, with one dirtied side. It also happens to fit neatly inside his stovepipe hat. He once apologized to a legal client for failing to respond to a letter because it was in an old hat in his closet rather than the new hat he was wearing.

Certainly Lincoln expressed variations on this note's concept for many years, including in the face-offs against Douglas. He liked to rail against "the Democracy," a generic term then in use for any government led by the Democratic Party, or for the party itself. Lincoln played on the multiple meanings of the word, and one of the principal definitions he has left us with is this: that neither slaves nor masters exist by law in a democracy. ∽

As I would not be a slave, so I would not be a master— This expresses my idea of democracy— Whatever differs from this, to the extent of the difference, is no democracy—

August 1858

70

"A Worthy Man"

A Recommendation for William Johnson

1862

WILLIAM JOHNSON WAS A BLACK MAN WHO CAME TO WORK FOR THE Lincolns in Springfield in early 1860. Such was his personal importance to the president-elect that he accompanied the family party on the inaugural train to Washington a year later, and was probably the only person not in the official political or military party to do so. Johnson was Lincoln's valet or "body servant" and was also Lincoln's ear when it came to black opinion. Though illiterate, he would hear talk that neither the press nor public officials would have access to. Elizabeth Keckly, Mary Lincoln's dressmaker and eventual confidante, is a much better-known example of this type of relationship, an interracial alliance not based on equality but firmly grounded in trust.

Johnson was prevented from working daily in the Executive Mansion, because the Irish and mulatto staff, as Lincoln soon put it, "would not have him" due to his dark skin. He came regularly nonetheless to cut the president's hair, trim his beard, and share news. He accompanied Lincoln to Antietam in 1862 and to Gettysburg in 1863. He died of smallpox in January 1864, apparently contracted from either Tad, Abraham, or someone in the crowds at Gettysburg. Lincoln paid for his burial at Arlington National Cemetery, where the marker today reads, "William H. Johnson, Citizen."

The five-dollar personal check shown here could have been given to Johnson for his regular duties, or perhaps to help with Tad in the period after Willie died and Mary was locked in her bedroom inconsolable. The simple card bearing the words, "The bearer of this, William Johnson (colored) came with me from Illinois, and is a worthy man, as I believe" was used by Johnson to get messenger or other work, most likely at the Treasury or Navy departments where blacks had historically been more welcome than elsewhere in the executive branch.

On that same day in 1862, Lincoln tried to prod General McClellan to pick up and capture Robert E. Lee after his Union's tactical victory at Antietam. While giving his personal protection to one black man, Lincoln simultaneously tried to effect a grand strategy of ending the fugitive status of millions like Johnson. The first goal he could manage alone; the second took cooperation from others not often willing to help. ∽

The bearer of this, William Johnson (colored) came with me from Illinois; and is a worthy man, as I believe.

Oct. 24, 1862   A. Lincoln

No. 80.   WASHINGTON D.C.   March 11.   1862

Riggs & Co.

Lith by HATCH & Cº 29 William St. N.Y

Pay to William Johnson (colored) — or bearer

Five — Dollars

$5

A. Lincoln.

71 One National Home

The Emancipation Proclamation

JANUARY 1, 1863

THE PRESIDENTIAL LIBRARY WAS GIVEN THIS DOCUMENT IN 1937 BY A wealthy Chicago collector. Someone may have purchased a humble home for the amount (three thousand dollars) another copy sold for in the same decade. In 2013, another copy of this same historic document sold for nearly two million dollars. The old expression that a house is the best investment might not have been true in this case.

Metaphors involving houses are apt for Lincoln's war-torn era. Thousands of southerners returned home at the war's end to find no home or family left. The same plight affected many in the ravaged border states too, and northerners felt the pinch of inflation and shortages of goods. Lincoln in 1858 had spoken of a "house divided," predicting that the nation could not last the way it was, half slave and half free, and he proved correct.

If the nation was by one conception a national family, sharing a continental home by 1860, it ought not to have been torn asunder. Lincoln's ploy to reunite it came with this document, by declaring the slaves—the family members, according to the census—of the rebels to be free people. He then worked politically, whether outwardly or behind the scenes, to prevent those freed people from ever being re-enslaved, and this whether his party won re-election or not. "And the promise being made, must be kept," he wrote in the Conkling letter (see pages 84–85).

We prize this treasure not because it is unique, for there are twenty-seven known copies of it signed by Lincoln, Secretary of State William Seward, and Lincoln's private secretary John G. Nicolay. We cannot prize the original manuscript of Emancipation in Lincoln's hand, because that burned in the Chicago Fire of 1871, where it was on display after being purchased during the war at a charity fair to aid wounded soldiers and their families. So too were these printed-and-signed copies sold at auction for the same noble purpose, probably for ten or fifteen dollars each. There are thought to have been forty-eight such copies on offer, so in theory twenty-one are still to be found by some lucky attic browsers. More concretely, emancipating the slaves in 1863 started the rapid process of giving all African Americans equal rights with whites, which was accomplished in about eight years. We are now one true family, with one national home. ⌒⌒

BY THE PRESIDENT OF THE UNITED STATES OF AMERICA.

A Proclamation.

......

Whereas, on the twenty-second day of September, in the year of our Lord one thousand eight hundred and sixty-two, a proclamation was issued by the President of the United States, containing, among other things, the following, to wit:

"That on the first day of January, in the year of our Lord one thousand eight hundred and sixty-three, all persons held as slaves within any State or designated part of a State, the people whereof shall then be in rebellion against the United States, shall be then, thenceforward, and forever, free; and the Executive government of the United States, including the military and naval authority thereof, will recognize and maintain the freedom of such persons, and will do no act or acts to repress such persons, or any of them, in any efforts they may make for their actual freedom.

"That the Executive will, on the first day of January aforesaid, by proclamation, designate the States and parts of States, if any, in which the people thereof, respectively, shall then be in rebellion against the United States; and the fact that any State, or the people thereof, shall on that day be in good faith represented in the Congress of the United States, by members chosen thereto at elections wherein a majority of the qualified voters of such State shall have participated, shall, in the absence of strong countervailing testimony, be deemed conclusive evidence that such State, and the people thereof, are not then in rebellion against the United States."

Now, therefore, I, ABRAHAM LINCOLN, PRESIDENT OF THE UNITED STATES, by virtue of the power in me vested as commander-in-chief of the army and navy of the United States, in time of actual armed rebellion against the authority and government of the United States, and as a fit and necessary war measure for suppressing said rebellion, do, on this first day of January, in the year of our Lord one thousand eight hundred and sixty-three, and in accordance with my purpose so to do, publicly proclaimed for the full period of one hundred days from the day first above mentioned, order and designate as the States and parts of States wherein the people thereof, respectively, are this day in rebellion against the United States, the following, to wit: ARKANSAS, TEXAS, LOUISIANA, (except the Parishes of St. Bernard, Plaquemines, Jefferson, St. John, St. Charles, St. James, Ascension, Assumption, Terre Bonne, Lafourche, St. Mary, St. Martin, and Orleans, including the City of New Orleans,) MISSISSIPPI, ALABAMA, FLORIDA, GEORGIA, SOUTH CAROLINA, NORTH CAROLINA, AND VIRGINIA, (except the forty-eight counties designated as West Virginia, and also the counties of Berkeley, Accomac, Northampton, Elizabeth City, York, Princess Ann, and Norfolk, including the cities of Norfolk and Portsmouth,) and which excepted parts are for the present left precisely as if this proclamation were not issued.

And by virtue of the power and for the purpose aforesaid, I do order and declare that all persons held as slaves within said designated States and parts of States are and henceforward shall be free; and that the Executive government of the United States, including the military and naval authorities thereof, will recognize and maintain the freedom of said persons.

And I hereby enjoin upon the people so declared to be free to abstain from all violence, unless in necessary self-defence; and I recommend to them that, in all cases when allowed, they labor faithfully for reasonable wages.

And I further declare and make known that such persons, of suitable condition, will be received into the armed service of the United States, to garrison forts, positions, stations, and other places, and to man vessels of all sorts in said service.

And upon this act, sincerely believed to be an act of justice warranted by the Constitution upon military necessity, I invoke the considerate judgment of mankind and the gracious favor of Almighty God.

In witness whereof I have hereunto set my hand and caused the seal of the United States to be affixed.

[L. S.] Done at the CITY OF WASHINGTON this first day of January, in the year of our Lord one thousand eight hundred and sixty-three, and of the Independence of the United States of America the eighty-seventh.

By the President: *Abraham Lincoln*

William H. Seward Secretary of State.

A true copy, with the autograph signatures of the President and the Secretary of State.

Jno. G. Nicolay Priv. Sec. to the President.

72 Commemorating History

The Emancipation Proclamation Pen

1863

As the American presidency has evolved, so too has the custom of signing proclamations and legislation. It is generally believed that Harry S Truman began the custom whereby a US president uses multiple pens to sign his name so that afterward he can hand the pen to several individuals who were instrumental in getting the legislation passed. The custom continues to this day, so much so, that a bill that would have taken Abraham Lincoln mere seconds to sign into law now takes several minutes.

Take for example the signing of the Civil Rights Act of 1964, which would not have been possible without "The Great Emancipator"'s issuance of the Emancipation Proclamation and the subsequent passage of the Thirteenth Amendment that ended slavery and involuntary servitude in the United States. President Lyndon B. Johnson was said to have signed the historic civil rights document using more than seventy pens.

A century and one year previously, Abraham Lincoln signed the Emancipation Proclamation with just one pen. As history tells it, he had been shaking a lot of hands earlier in the day and was fearful that this might cause him to sign the historic document in a weakened fashion. He thought that anything less than a firm signature might suggest he was hesitant about what he was signing even if it was his very own proclamation. In the end, he set forth his signature in a confident manner, then said aloud, "I never, in my life, felt more certain that I was doing right, than I do in signing this paper."

Were it like the twenty-first century, he might have handed a commemorative pen to Secretary of State William Seward, whose name also appears on the historic document. Instead, Lincoln and Seward signed a number of commemorative printed copies using a different pen. Attested to by Mary Lincoln, this pen is the one her husband used to sign the commemorative copies. It is now a treasured artifact in the ALPLM's collection. Made by American manufacturer C. Parker circa 1860, it has a wooden black-lacquered barrel with a silver inlaid grip section that leads to its nib (now missing). The pen is accompanied by a silvered metal inlaid case, elliptical in shape. Records tell us that forty-eight copies of the commemorative document were signed, all presumably on one day, by one man, using one pen. ☍

I never, in my life, felt more certain that I was doing right, than I do in signing this paper.—A. LINCOLN UPON SIGNING THE EMANCIPATION PROCLAMATION

Washington, Jan. 18. 1865

F. P. Blair, Esq

Sir:

Your having shown
me Mr. Davis' letter to you of
the 12th. Inst., you may say to
him that I have constantly been,
am now, and shall continue,
ready to receive any agent
whom he, or any other influential person now resisting the national authority, may informally
send to me, with the view of
securing peace to the people of
our one common country,

Yours &c

A. Lincoln.

"Our One Common Country"

Slave-Free

JANUARY 18, 1865

73

NEVER BUDGE, NEVER GIVE IN. THIS COULD BE THE WRONG APPROACH for many a negotiation. Yet in the case of the Lincoln Administration's stance on slavery, by 1863 nearly all seven Cabinet members were resolved to stand firm, and by the time of Lincoln's re-election in November 1864, even with a pair of newcomers, it was a determined group. Lincoln was perhaps the most determined of all.

Still, the bloodshed was crushing Lincoln's spirit. He approached Francis Preston Blair Sr., as veteran a politico as could be found, to enter into secret negotiations with Confederate officials at the highest level to try to bring an early end to the war. But under no circumstance would the war end without slavery's end, simultaneously. Why secret? Because radicals in and out of Congress could not brook the idea of speaking to the rebels at any level; Lincoln would be seen as soft if he did so. Therefore, a cross-party hand like Blair, who had served in Andrew Jackson's Cabinet as a Democrat, and who was the father of Lincoln's former Republican postmaster-general, Montgomery Blair, might act as bridge. The Blairs had been substantial Maryland slave owners yet remained loyal to the Union. Lincoln suspected rightly that leading Virginians might listen.

They did, to a point. Recognizing "our one common country" was the second stipulation that Lincoln put upon the "peace talks." The first was "an end to slavery." But Jefferson Davis, even after more than two hundred thousand Confederate deaths, and the crushing of the cotton economy and social life of the southern states by late 1864, would not budge. His watchword was "never give in," and so he both declined to meet Lincoln personally and declined to acknowledge the two plain terms. He sent R. M. T. Hunter, John C. Campbell, and his vice president Alexander Stephens, to meet Lincoln and William H. Seward on February 2, 1865, to debate whether some slaves could be kept, and whether some dim states' rights could be preserved. About five hours of talk ensued, with no settlement.

Thus, the war continued for another three months. Tens of thousands more northern and southern men were killed, and Lincoln himself was killed. One country emerged, slave-free. ∞

74 From Struggle to Souvenir

The Thirteenth Amendment

JANUARY 31, 1865

THERE HAVE BEEN NO SOUVENIR VERSIONS OF ANY OTHER AMENDMENT to the US Constitution than the Thirteenth. Perhaps this is because the origins of the Thirteenth Amendment are what founded a political party, and completed a Union in which "all men are created equal." Since 1776 antislavery movements had burned at different temperatures, from mild concern to all-out hatred of the institution for either religious, economic, political, or constitutional reasons. The Republican Party arose in 1854 from the disarray of the Whig party in order to bring the stronger antislavery elements together. Lincoln did not join right away, as an antislavery stance was a losing one for politicians in most of Illinois—and in most states—at that time.

His and the nation's rapidly changing views on human equality, civil rights, and perhaps most of all the recognition of the slave system's barbarity led Lincoln out on a dangerous limb with his 1863 Emancipation Proclamation (see pages 152–53). The full-bore civil expression of that movement took form in 1864 when the US Senate, and Lincoln supporting, resolved to amend the Constitution permanently, rather than try to build further statutory or judicial fences around the slave power.

The passage of a parallel resolution through the more democratic and Democratic House of Representatives was harder. Steven Spielberg's film *Lincoln* dramatizes that effort, which bore fruit on January 31, 1865. A majority of two votes came as a surprise, followed by jubilation. Immediately the resolution went out to the states for ratification (three-fourths of them being necessary). Illinois was number one, on the very next day. Georgia made number twenty-seven (of the thirty-six states), on December 6, 1865.

Back in the House, the souvenir copies went flying from desk to desk. Today fifteen are known to exist, aside from the short, legal document in the National Archives that bears only five signatures. On only three of the fifteen did Lincoln sign and add the date of February 1, 1865, above the long lists of congressional signatures. Those in the long column at left are senators; the other three columns are representatives. Such was the flurry of activity that on the ALPLM's copy, three of the representatives signed it twice, in different columns. This one also bears another presidential signature: James Garfield's (column 3, about halfway down) representing his Ohio district at the time.

Graphic Conservation Company of Chicago performed *pro bono* work on this delicate treasure in 2011, stabilizing the inks and the vellum and making it live anew for the eyes of future generations. ᏉᎠ

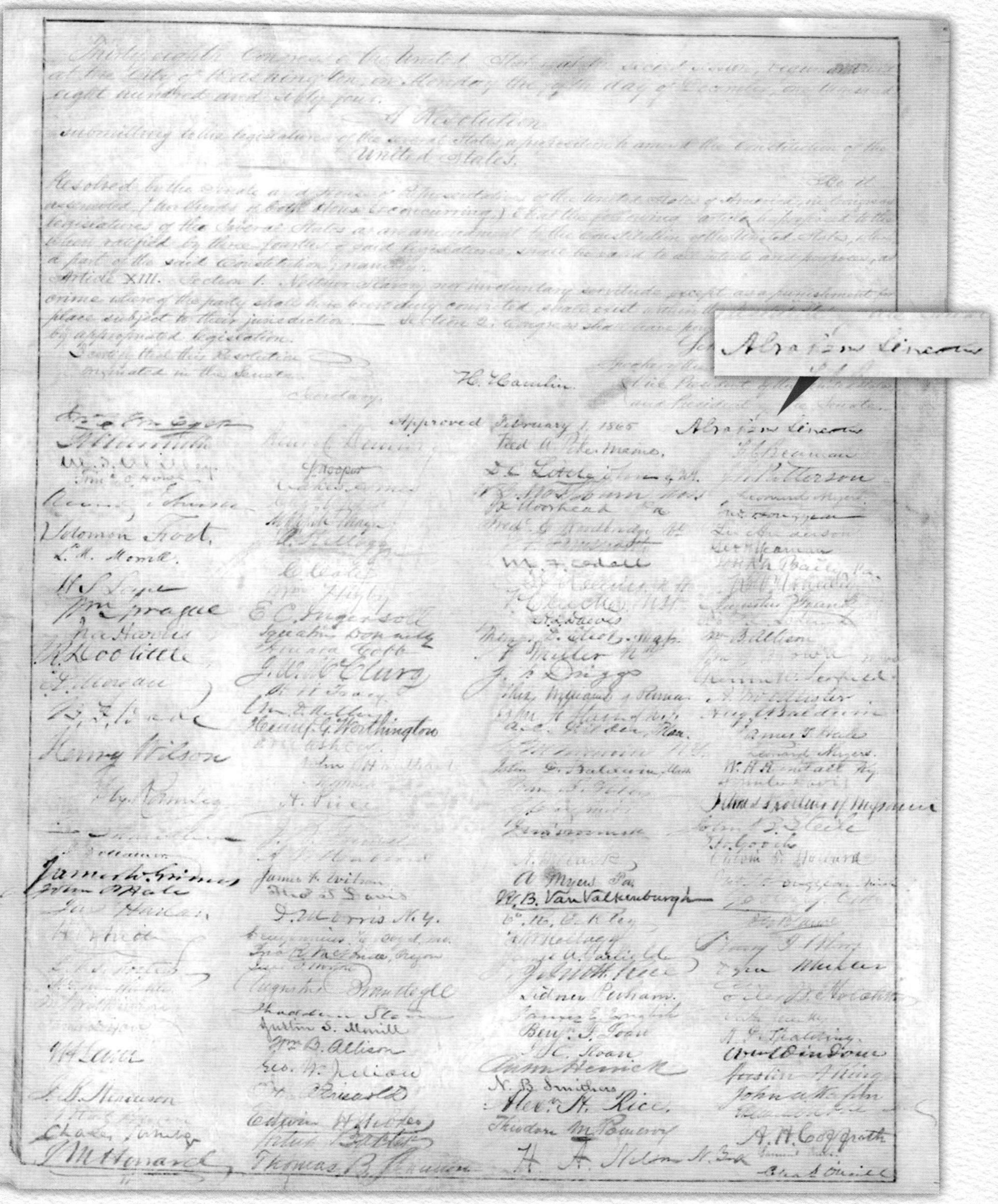
Thirty-eighth Congress of the United States of America; at the second session, begun and held at the City of Washington, on Monday, the fifth day of December, one thousand eight hundred and sixty-four.

A Resolution

submitting to the legislatures of the several States a proposition to amend the Constitution of the United States.

Resolved by the Senate and House of Representatives of the United States of America in Congress assembled (two thirds of both houses concurring) that the following article be proposed to the legislatures of the several States as an amendment to the Constitution of the United States, which, when ratified by three fourths of said legislatures, shall be valid to all intents and purposes, as a part of the said Constitution, namely: Article XIII. Section 1. Neither slavery nor involuntary servitude, except as a punishment for crime whereof the party shall have been duly convicted, shall exist within the United States, or any place subject to their jurisdiction. Section 2. Congress shall have power to enforce this article by appropriate legislation.

I certify that this Resolution originated in the Senate.

Secretary

Speaker of the House of Representatives

H. Hamlin

Vice President of the United States and President of the Senate

Approved February 1. 1865

Abraham Lincoln

Solomon Foot.

Henry Wilson

E. C. Ingersoll

Henry G. Worthington

W. B. Van Valkenburgh

A. Myers

Sidney Perham

Benj. F. Loan

Alex. H. Rice

Edwin H. Webster

Thomas B. Shannon

A. H. Coffroth

75 Chaos of a Collapsing Rebellion

A Cotton Permit Is Issued

MARCH 1865

SOME RADICALS SOUGHT TO SNUFF OUT THE ENTIRE SOUTHERN ECONomy. Lincoln felt that the widows of rebel cotton-growers, or their children, for example, ought not necessarily be starved out, and that goods legally taken in the war could enter the market. The chase for permits to legally sell captured cotton in the last months of the war was fierce, and unquestionably there were semi-legal or illegal actions, usually by unsupervised Union men or their sutlers (civilian merchants who sold provisions to armies in the field). Here Lincoln signed a proper one for Charles E. Fuller to sell ten thousand bales to Hanson A. Risley at Norfolk, Virginia, before the end of 1865.

The sixteenth president may have been criticized for lending a little more aid of this type to relatives of Mary Lincoln, or to particular political or military friends. He worked as best he could with the Treasury Department, which actually wrote the rules, and with Congress, which either enforced or revised the rules. Lincoln's focus in 1865 was to ensure the continued freedom of the freed people; to get loyalists old or new into positions of authority in the seceded states so that they could be re-admitted to Congress as quickly as possible; and to return the Union to the *status quo ante*, with the enormous exception that slavery would be gone. Lincoln's own disinterest in money and material things probably blinded him at times to the large amounts of it that some people, men or women, were grabbing up in the chaos of a collapsing rebellion. ∽

I think I have no prejudice against the southern people. They are just what we would be in their situation.
—ABRAHAM LINCOLN AT PEORIA ON OCTOBER 16, 1854

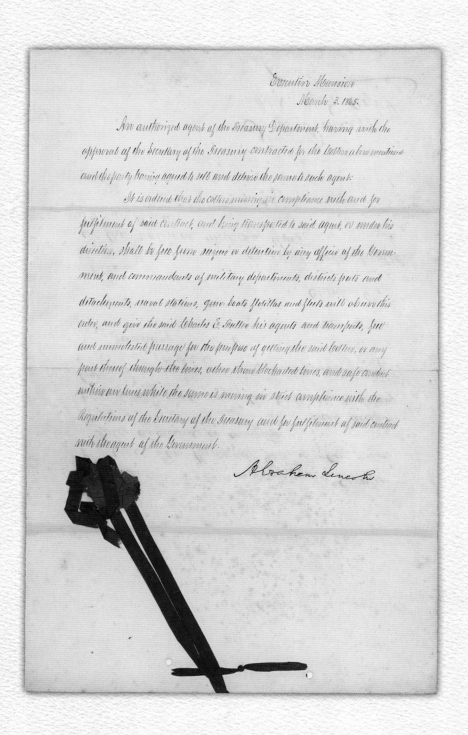

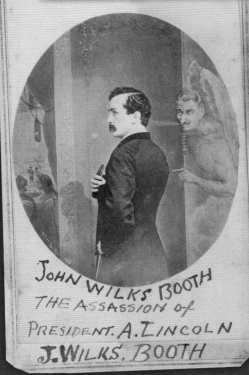

JOHN WILKS BOOTH
THE ASSASSIN of
PRESIDENT. A. LINCOLN
J. WILKS, BOOTH

Top: Springfield mourners line up to pay their respects; official announcement of President Lincoln's death.
Bottom: John Wilkes Booth is demonized; President Lincoln's Springfield home is draped with funerary bunting and his horse, "Old Bob," wears a mourning blanket.

PART 7
❧ MARTYR ❧

A. Lincoln

76

Love-Struck and Cold-Blooded

Lincoln's Assassin

1864

LEE HARVEY OSWALD, LEON CZOLGOSZ, CHARLES GUITEAU, JOHN Wilkes Booth: These are the assassins of Presidents Kennedy, McKinley, Garfield, and Lincoln. It is difficult to think of any assassin in human terms—to associate words like thoughtfulness, tenderness, and love with those who so callously and calculatingly ended the life of another. Still, thoughtfulness, tenderness, and love are exactly the words associated with John Wilkes Booth when one beholds the letters and pearl promise ring the Confederate sympathizer and Lincoln assassin gave to the young Isabel Sumner in the summer of 1864.

Five-foot-eight-inches tall with strapping good looks, Booth was a famous actor of the time and popular with the ladies. Although he could probably attract the girl of his choosing, it seems his heart was lost to the seventeen-year-old Bostonian. While it is uncertain how they met, it most probably occurred during a theatrical run Booth had at the Boston Museum. It seems at least for the renowned actor it was the pro-verbial "love at first sight." Booth said in a letter to Sumner, "I saw you, things seemed to change." Booth showered Sumner with letters and signed a photograph of himself, "yours with affection J. Wilkes Booth."

A more public example of his love and affection came in the form of a pearl ring, which Booth gave to the young beauty. The gold ring's pearl is set in a floret design and surrounded with gemstones. The inside of the band is inscribed: "J.W.B. to I.S." Booth had chosen a pearl, the symbol of purity and innocence, as the symbol of his love. Some nine months later, after Lincoln's assassination and his own subsequent death, most individuals who had ties to him destroyed anything they may have owned which linked them together, doing so either out of fear of association or disgust for his dastardly deed. Women with whom he had corresponded and possibly dated burned his letters. That is, seemingly all women but one, Isabel Sumner, who not only saved the letters and photographs, but the ring as well. It is unclear whether she did so out of love, sentimentality, or for posterity, but the items survive to this day having been passed down through Sumner family members and then eventually sold as the historic collectibles they are. The items, most notably the ring, provide a rare glimpse into the personal life of this love-struck actor turned cold-blooded killer—Lincoln's assassin. The purity and innocence of the pearl forever contrast with the evil treacherousness of its villainous bestower. ᴄ

77

A Night at the Theater

Our American Cousin

1865

THEATERGOER MR. J. CRAFT BOUGHT TWO "SPECIAL SEATS" FOR THE benefit performance of *Our American Cousin* being performed at Ford's Theatre on Friday, April 14, 1865. Not only was it an opportunity to see "distinguished manageress, authoress and actress" Laura Keene, as she was billed in the amply distributed playbills, it was an opportunity to see, firsthand, the president and Mrs. Lincoln, also in attendance. Craft had secured seats 42 and 43 in the Orchestra section—the section closest to the stage and just to the lower left of the presidential box. It is possible that Craft passed through the Orchestra section and moved to special seats in a private box, because his tickets were white, a color Ford's used to designate seats in private boxes. In any case, Craft and his guest would have a good view of both the stage and the presidential box located stage left. On his arrival, he and his guest would have entered theater door Number 2—the same door through which the presidential entourage came in after the play had already begun.

When orchestra director William Withers realized that the president had arrived, he directed the musicians to play "Hail to the Chief," after which the performance resumed. At the midpoint of Act III, Scene 2, the character of Asa Trenchard played by Harry Hawk regales two characters about his ability to shoot. Although he refers to bows and arrows, the dialogue suddenly becomes eerily prescient and strangely prophetic.

> ASA TRENCHARD: "Wal, I guess shooting . . . is just about like most things in life, all you've got to do is keep the sun out of your eyes, look straight—pull strong—calculate the distance and you're sure to hit the mark in most things as well as shooting."

As the line was being delivered, John Wilkes Booth was making his way toward the presidential box to assassinate President Lincoln. Within minutes, Booth looked straight, calculated the distance, pulled strong, and fatefully hit his mark. Mr. Craft and his guest's special evening at the theater had suddenly and violently ended, no doubt indelibly etched into their memories forever. Their commander-in-chief, whom they had hailed a little more than an hour earlier, was now on his final march home. ∽

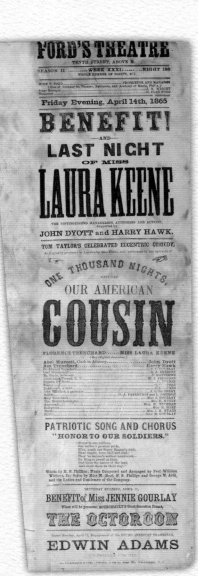

Original playbill for the fateful performance of *Our American Cousin* at which Abraham Lincoln was assassinated

Ticket for the April 14, 1865 performance of *Our American Cousin* at Ford's Theatre and the Presidential Box

78

Backstory of a Chair

The Ford's Theatre Rush Seat

At first glance, the chair shown here looks rather ordinary with its black ebonized frame and rush seat. But the backstory reveals that this was one of the original chairs at Ford's Theatre on the night of Abraham Lincoln's assassination. Approximately sixteen hundred people attended the performance of *Our American Cousin* that evening on April 14, 1865. While some sat in chairs, others sat on benches, depending upon the ticket price they paid: twenty-five cents in the Family Circle, one dollar for the Orchestra section, six dollars for a lower box, and ten dollars for an upper box, which is where Lincoln watched the performance. Although not as ornate as the plush red damask rocking chair, part of the permanent collection of the Henry Ford Museum, in which the president sat, the chair pictured here has historic value nonetheless.

The black frame chair in the ALPLM's collection is one of only five surviving today. The other four from the orchestra level of the theater are part of the permanent collection of the Chicago History Museum. No boxes other than the presidential box were occupied that evening. Mr. and Mrs. Lincoln were joined in their state box by Major Henry Rathbone and his fiancée Clara Harris. The Lincolns had invited their son Robert, as well as Ulysses S. Grant and his wife Julia, but none were able to attend. Given the known facts, it is likely that the black frame chair was occupied by someone who attended the show that night specifically to see the Lincolns or the Grants.

The devastating events of April 14, 1865, left a nation and its people scarred. Near the tenth anniversary of the event, Mary Lincoln's behavior became so erratic and self-endangering that she was committed to an asylum by a jury in Chicago and then released four months later to live out her life just as unhappily. And while Henry Rathbone and Clara Harris eventually married, Henry could never get over his inability to protect the president—a reality that ultimately drove him to madness. In the end, Rathbone murdered his wife and was also committed to an asylum, in Germany, where he died. ∽

How many more martyrs to slavery?
—*Theatergoer* Frederick A. Sawyer

79

Grim Yet Cherished Reminders

A Fateful Night

1865

ON THE EVENING OF APRIL 14, 1865, ABRAHAM AND MARY LINCOLN left the White House for Ford's Theatre, a relatively short trip via carriage. It was not the first time they had traveled there. Fond of the theater, the Lincolns attended about ten theatrical performances at Ford's over the course of the presidency. On this particular evening, they were going to see the closing performance of the British comedic play *Our American Cousin*. It had been widely publicized that the President and Mrs. Lincoln would attend, as would General and Julia Grant. But the Grants were unable to make it, nor was the Lincolns' eldest son Robert, whom they also had asked to join them. In the end, Major Henry Rathbone, who had seen action at the battles of Antietam and Fredricksburg, and his fiancée Clara Harris joined the Lincolns for the performance.

My husband's blood. My dear husband's blood. —MARY LINCOLN

The president was wearing his customary black suit; Mary, a black silk gown with a floral design and matching bonnet. Like most ladies of the day, she carried a retractable fan. The fan was no doubt the height of fashion of the time, made of silk with ostrich-feathers decorating the tip of each blade. The fan's frame was made of carved ivory with a tassel strung to its base for easy carrying. The Lincolns looked very smart as they entered the presidential box. The play, which had already begun, was paused for a moment, as "Hail to the Chief" was played and an air of excitement filled the theater.

Major Rathbone and Clara Harris moved into the box and sat to the right of the first lady. The president sat to her left nearest the entry door. The performance resumed, and soon came that fateful moment when assassin John Wilkes Booth entered the box and pointed his .44 derringer pistol at the president's head and fired. Major Rathbone sprang from his seat in an attempt to restrain the president's assassin. When he did so, Rathbone's arm was deeply sliced by Booth, who had dropped his gun and pulled out a dagger to slash himself free from the major's grasp. In the tumult of the moment, Mary's dress and fan were stained with blood, most likely Rathbone's. These stains are visible to this day. After the assassination of her husband, Mary Lincoln never attended the theater again. ∽

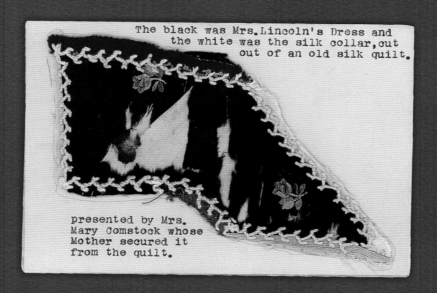

The black was Mrs. Lincoln's Dress and the white was the silk collar, cut out of an old silk quilt.

presented by Mrs. Mary Comstock whose Mother secured it from the quilt.

A Presidential Pocket

Its Final Contents

1865

ON THE EVENING OF APRIL 14, 1865, ABRAHAM LINCOLN WAS IN AN upbeat mood. The end of the war was imminent. Congress had passed his resolution to permanently end slavery and involuntary servitude in the United States and its possessions. After a long day of work that included a Cabinet meeting with an appearance by General Grant, Lincoln prepared to attend a performance of *Our American Cousin* at Ford's Theatre. He was not especially keen on going but felt duty-bound to attend, since he had promised he would and his attendance had been publicized. He readied himself for the evening, filling his pockets with his handkerchief, two pairs of spectacles and a lens polisher, a pocket knife, newspaper clippings, a five-dollar Confederate note he had obtained during his recent visit to Richmond, and a watch fob. He also took with him a pair of white kid gloves.

It was customary in the nineteenth century for both women and men to wear gloves, not only for warmth, but for more formal social occasions like attending the theater. The president most likely wore the gloves to the theater and then removed them on arrival, placing them neatly folded in the left hand pocket of his coat.

When the fateful shot rang out and the mortally wounded president's blood began to flow, some of it found its way to his gloves. The deep crimson color of the blood, now a faded brown, rests in stark contrast to the cream color of the kidskin. These gloves are now a somber, yet cherished artifact in the ALPLM's collection.

Mary Lincoln kept the gloves along with the handkerchief for approximately three years before she gave or sold the items to Captain Benjamin Richardson, a well-known collector of historic artifacts and presidential ephemera. The artifacts were delivered to Richardson by the Lincolns' son Tad, who was living with his mother Mary in Chicago at that time. The gloves are a grisly reminder of the day America, indeed the world, lost one of the greatest leaders in its history. ∽

The shrill cry of murder from Mrs. Lincoln first roused the horrified audience . . . The silence of death was broken by shouts of "kill him" and strong men wept, and cursed, and tore the seats in the impotence of their anger. —Theatergoer JAMES KNOX

Valiant but Failed Efforts

A Somber Keepsake

1865

ABRAHAM LINCOLN WAS NOT KNOWN AS ONE TO GET CAUGHT UP IN appearances, especially his own. He was known on occasion to answer the door in his stocking feet with his suspenders hanging at his sides. When Lincoln visited the temporary studio in Urbana, Illinois, of photographer Samuel Alschuler, Alschuler was disappointed to see that Lincoln was informally dressed and so he offered his own black coat to Lincoln, who graciously agreed to wear it. The coat was obviously too small for Lincoln, who was almost a foot taller than the photographer, and its sleeves were far too short. Lincoln paid no mind and sat for the photo. It is no surprise that as Lincoln ascended to the presidency, the quality of his clothing and state of dress improved. Mary Lincoln no doubt had an influence on what her husband wore, and, even more so, what he would no longer wear. Clearly this was the case on the night of the performance at Ford's Theatre. Lincoln entered wearing a fine black suit consisting of frock and waist coats, trousers, shirt, tie, and boots. His overcoat was made by the renowned American clothier Brooks Brothers; his stovepipe hat of silk was made by Washington milliner J. Y. Davis. A cherished piece of the Abraham Lincoln Presidential Library and Museum is a small cuff button from the sleeve of the shirt the president was wearing the night of the assassination. The handsome button is ornately designed gold with inset black enamel in which the gold letter "L" is set in a Gothic script.

The button had been removed by Dr. Charles Sabin Taft, who was at Ford's Theatre the night of the assassination and was one of a handful of medical professionals who eventually attended to the president. Taft removed the button in an effort to search Lincoln's body for any additional wounds. After the president's death, Mary Lincoln gave the button to Dr. Taft in gratitude for his valiant, but failed efforts. Some thirty-five years after the assassination, Taft wrote an affidavit attesting to the provenance of the button. ∞

This cuff button, with the letter 'L' set in black enamel was removed by me from President Lincoln's cuff, when taking off his shirt in the box at Ford's Theater, the night he was assassinated April 14 1865 I Charles Sabin Taft . . . N.Y. / June 30 1900.

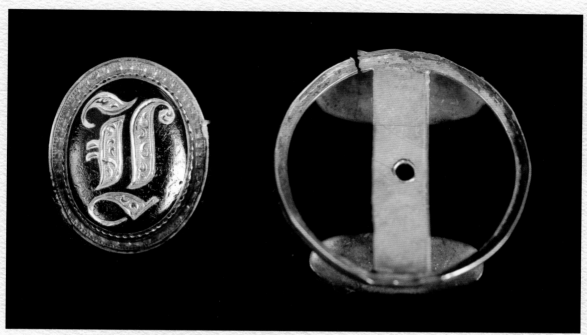

MR. LINCOLN IN 1857.

Photograph by Samuel
Alschuler of Lincoln wearing
the photographer's coat

82

Awaiting Her Cue

Laura Keene's Date with Destiny

1865

LAURA KEENE, BORN MARY FRANCES MOSS, WAS A RENOWNED nineteenth-century British actress and theater manager known as much, if not more, for her astute managerial abilities as for her considerable talents as an actress. On the evening of April 14, 1865, Keene co-starred in a performance of the play *Our American Cousin*, the final show in a two-week run in Washington, DC, from which a portion of the box-office receipts would go directly to her.

Keene, who had once dated actor Edwin Booth, older brother of John Wilkes Booth, played the lead female role of Florence Trenchard. In the midst of the performance, midway into Act III, Scene 2, actor Harry Hawk, playing the male lead of Asa Trenchard, the "American cousin," recites the line, "Don't know the manners of good society, eh? Well, I guess I know enough to turn you inside out, old gal—you sockdologizing old man-trap." The line elicited raucous laughter from the audience while a shot rang out from the presidential box. The president's assassin escaped by leaping to the stage and riding off on horseback into the cool spring night. Keene was awaiting her cue to enter the scene just after Hawk finished his lines. Instead, in the midst of the mayhem, she bravely rushed to the presidential box just above her, only to find the president lying helpless and unconscious. She asked the doctors if she could cradle the head of the dying president while they attended to him. Because of the severity of the wound, an ample amount of blood stained the actress's dress.

Lincoln sadly never regained consciousness. But in those frenzied moments after the fatal wound was inflicted, Laura Keene displayed compassion and tenderness toward the savior of the Union as he began his final journey home that Good Friday evening.

A piece of Keene's dress is now a part of the ALPLM's collection. About a year after that indelible experience, Keene herself gave this piece of the keepsake to the builders of Lincoln's tomb in Springfield, Illinois. The dress fragment, once a piece of a costume, now a piece of history, is a tragic reminder of that foreordained moment when the stage went dark, as did the world. ∽

A swatch of Laura Keene's costume stained with the blood of Abraham Lincoln

83

Shock and Awe

The New York Daily News's *Report*

APRIL 15, 1865

A MAJORITY OF THE NEWSPAPERS IN NEW YORK CITY WERE ANTI-Lincoln, because a majority of the residents were. Much acclaim has come down over the years to Horace Greeley of the *Tribune*, Henry Raymond of the *Times*, and James Gordon Bennett of the *Herald* as operators of the three largest dailies that were also more or less supportive of the administration (though Bennett's *Herald* always stood athwart the black man's interest and dignity, while Raymond did not like the idea of black soldiers). On balance, the city supported the Union war effort, grew to accept black rights, and gradually warmed to Lincoln himself.

But not the *Daily News*, and not a half-dozen other smaller papers. Its editor, Benjamin Wood, a Democratic congressman for Manhattan, never spent time in Fort Lafayette as did a few of the other scurrilous and semi-treasonous Democratic editors, but the *Daily News* wrote such nuggets in the long "Federal Nursery Rhyme" as this couplet:

> *Seward in the Cabinet*
> *surrounded by his spies;*
> *Halleck with the telegraph*
> *Busy forging lies . . .*

Because this kind of "free press" was deemed sympathetic to the enemy and endangering to the troops by a grand jury, Postmaster-General Montgomery Blair barred a half-dozen titles from the US mails in 1861. The *Daily News* held on to the notion that the South would never be conquered, and that Lincoln was reveling in a "carnival of slaughter." Wood and his brother Fernando, mayor of New York in 1861 and 1862, were leaders of the movement against the Thirteenth Amendment.

Yet the honorable thing for the *News* to do when the president was shot was to magnify its front page in the same way that all other newspapers did. The reportage continued all night, with most papers printing more than one edition (the *Herald* printed six) before Andrew Johnson was sworn in at 10:00 a.m. on Saturday, April 15. Stacked headlines in the first column that summarize the main event had become standard by about 1850, yet rarely did so many words of shock and awe get piled one on top of another. Antiwar or pro-Confederate northerners were right that "Horror Upon Horror" described the war years, but the phrase also told of one night's events, in which rumors still swirled. ∞

NEW YORK DAILY NEWS.

VOL. IX.....NO. 80. NEW YORK, SATURDAY, APRIL 15, 1865. PRICE FOUR CENTS.

A TERRIBLE CRIME

THE PRESIDENT ASSASSINATED

A Pistol Ball Through His Head.

NOT EXPECTED TO LIVE.

Wild Excitement at Washington

THE ASSASSIN ESCAPES.

The Terrible Scene at the Theater

HORROR UPON HORROR

MR. SEWARD STABBED.

TWO DAYS LATER FROM EUROPE.

THE AFFAIR AT LISBON.

Reparation Demanded of Portugal.

PALMERSTON AND THE POPE.

MORE ENGLISH FAILURES

THE ATLANTIC TELEGRAPH

THE FRENCH OPPOSITION

PRESS REFORM DENIED.

NAPOLEON GOING TO RUSTICATE

THE POPE DENOUNCING MAXIMILIAN

The Prussian Parliamentary Struggle.

MEXICO.

A WHOLE ARMY ABANDONS JUAREZ.

84

Wanted Alive

The Hunt for the Conspirators

1865

ON APRIL 20, 1865, SIX DAYS AFTER LINCOLN AND SEWARD WERE attacked, the US War Department was still issuing wanted posters—calling for the apprehension of their assailants.

The ALPLM has two different posters issued at that time. The first prominently displays *carte-de-visite* photos actually affixed to the poster and announcing a one-hundred-thousand-dollar reward: fifty thousand for the plot's mastermind, John Wilkes Booth, and twenty-five thousand each for John Surratt and David Herold. In total, these rewards are equivalent to approximately four million dollars today.

Surratt, son of co-conspirator Mary Surratt, fled to Canada and then abroad to Rome. Herold and Booth remained at large until they were cornered in a Virginia tobacco barn on the property now infamously known as Garrett's Farm. In the early morning hours of April 26, 1865, Union soldiers of the 16th New York Cavalry surrounded Booth and Herold as they slept. Ultimately Herold surrendered, but Booth would not, so the soldiers set fire to the barn hoping to smoke him out. In the end, he came into custody only after he was shot, and he expired later that day. Herold surrendered and was eventually tried and executed with three of his fellow conspirators, Lewis Powell, George Atzerodt, and Mary Surratt—the first woman to be executed in the United States. John Surratt was extradited to the United States and tried in a Maryland civil court in 1867 but was eventually released after a mistrial was declared because of a hung jury. Seventy-five thousand dollars of the reward offered by the US War Department was awarded to a number of investigators and hunters including the twenty-six members of the cavalry who surrounded Garrett's barn and captured Booth and Herold. Because John Surratt was never captured, the twenty-five-thousand-dollar bounty on his head was never awarded.

A rarer poster places a thirty-thousand-dollar bounty on John Wilkes Booth's head and that of the then unknown co-conspirator, Lewis Powell, who attempted to assassinate Secretary of State William Seward. This reward was gathered and offered by Lafayette C. Baker, "colonel and agent" of the War Department brought in to help apprehend the assassins. It is unknown if the reward was ever paid, but Baker himself received a portion of the one-hundred-thousand-dollar reward offered by the War Department. While the reward amounts were unprecedented at the time, they were mere pittances considering the priceless, irreplaceable nature of the nation's fallen leader. ∽

SURRAT.   BOOTH.   HAROLD.

War Department, Washington, April 20, 1865,

$100,000 REWARD!

THE MURDERER

Of our late beloved President, Abraham Lincoln,

IS STILL AT LARGE.

$50,000 REWARD

Will be paid by this Department for his apprehension, in addition to any reward offered by Municipal Authorities or State Executives.

$25,000 REWARD

Will be paid for the apprehension of JOHN H. SURRATT, one of Booth's Accomplices.

$25,000 REWARD

Will be paid for the apprehension of David C. Harold, another of Booth's accomplices.

LIBERAL REWARDS will be paid for any information that shall conduce to the arrest of either of the above-named criminals, or their accomplices.

All persons harboring or secreting the said persons, or either of them, or aiding or assisting their concealment or escape, will be treated as accomplices in the murder of the President and the attempted assassination of the Secretary of State, and shall be subject to trial before a Military Commission and the punishment of DEATH.

Let the stain of innocent blood be removed from the land by the arrest and punishment of the murderers.

All good citizens are exhorted to aid public justice on this occasion. Every man should consider his own conscience charged with this solemn duty, and rest neither night nor day until it be accomplished.

EDWIN M. STANTON, Secretary of War.

DESCRIPTIONS.—BOOTH is Five Feet 7 or 8 inches high, slender build, high forehead, black hair, black eyes, and wears a heavy black moustache.

JOHN H. SURRAT is about 5 feet, 9 inches. Hair rather thin and dark; eyes rather light; no beard. Would weigh 145 or 150 pounds. Complexion rather pale and clear, with color in his cheeks. Wore light clothes of fine quality. Shoulders square; check bones rather prominent; chin narrow; ears projecting at the top; forehead rather low and square, but broad. Parts his hair on the right side; neck rather long. His lips are firmly set. A slim man.

DAVID C. HAROLD is five feet six inches high, hair dark, eyes dark, eyebrows rather heavy, full face, nose short, hand short and fleshy, feet small, instep high, round bodied, naturally quick and active, slightly closes his eyes when looking at a person.

NOTICE.—In addition to the above, State and other authorities have offered rewards amounting to almost one hundred thousand dollars, making an aggregate of about TWO HUNDRED THOUSAND DOLLARS.

$30,000 REWARD

DESCRIPTION

OF

JOHN WILKES BOOTH!

Who Assassinated the PRESIDENT on the Evening of April 14th, 1865.

Height 5 feet 8 inches; weight 160 pounds; compact built; hair jet black, inclined to curl, medium length, parted behind; eyes black, and heavy dark eye-brows; wears a large seal ring on little finger; when talking inclines his head forward; looks down.

Description of the Person who Attempted to Assassinate Hon. W. H. Seward, Secretary of State.

Height 6 feet 1 inch; hair black, thick, full and straight; no beard, nor appearance of beard; cheeks red on the jaws; face moderately full; 22 or 23 years of age; eyes, color not known—large eyes, not prominent; brows not heavy, but dark; face not large, but rather round; complexion healthy; nose straight and well formed, medium size; mouth small; lips thin; upper lip protruded when he talked; chin pointed and prominent; head medium size; neck short, and of medium length; hands soft and small; fingers tapering; shows no signs of hard labor; broad shoulders; taper waist; straight figure; strong looking man; manner not gentlemanly, but vulgar; Overcoat double-breasted, color mixed of pink and grey spots, small —was a sack overcoat, pockets in side and one on the breast, with lappells or flaps; pants black, common stuff; new heavy boots; voice small and thin, inclined to tenor.

The Common Council of Washington, D. C., have offered a reward of $20,000 for the arrest and conviction of these Assassins, in addition to which I will pay $10,000.

L. C. BAKER,
Colonel and Agent War Department.

85

Fragment of a Funeral

The Pink Marble Square

1865

At first glance, the thick, pink square looks like an ordinary piece of marble, but its unpolished underside tells the real story, for here a small typed note reads,

> From the table on which the Body of Abraham Lincoln lay after his assassination, during the trip from Washington, D.C., to Springfield, Illinois in a car of the Penn. R.R. April 15th, 1865

This was attested to by N. P. Brook, then the general manager of the Philadelphia Division of the Pennsylvania Railroad. The marble square is but one of several similar pieces which, when they once formed a whole table top, carried a divided nation's sacrificial offering in the form of its devoted martyr and fallen leader, Abraham Lincoln. The route of the funeral train, for the most part, reversed the journey he had taken more than four years earlier when he had left his beloved Springfield for Washington, DC, to assume the duties of commander-in-chief of the United States of America.

Lincoln's funeral train left Washington's Union Station on April 21, 1865, and arrived in Springfield, Illinois, on May 3, 1865. Over the course of its thirteen-day

journey, whether along the train route or at memorial services, approximately eight million people viewed and paid tribute to the fallen leader. Some of them saw Lincoln's coffin resting on the train's pink marble table when three brief stops were made that allowed the public to walk through the train car itself. The man had undergone a metamorphosis, from living mortal to slain immortal savior. His is considered to be the most attended funeral in history. And in the end, this simple pink square became part of the most celebrated pieces of marble ever.

Sometime after the funeral, the top of the pink marble table was cut up into four-by-six-inch sections like the one shown here. The squares were sold as souvenirs—a sadly irreverent end to something that played an integral part in our nation's most reverential moment. Still, the marble square preserves a piece of that history for all time. It is the only piece of the table known to exist in a public institution today. ∞

With the pomp of the inloop'd flags with the cities draped in black,
With the show of the States themselves as of crape-veil'd women standing,
With processions long and winding and the flambeaus of the night,
With the countless torches lit, with the silent sea of faces and the unbared heads,
With the waiting depot, the arriving coffin, and the sombre faces.
 —WALT WHITMAN, "WHEN LILACS LAST IN THE DOORYARD BLOOM'D"

Oh! why should the spirit of mortal be proud?
Like a swift-fleeting meteor, a fast-flying cloud
A flash of the lightning, a break of the wave
He passeth from life to his rest in the grave.
                                        —WILLIAM KNOX

The Only Print

Gurney Takes a Photo

1865

WHEN LINCOLN DIED IN THE EARLY MORNING HOURS OF SATURDAY, April 15, 1865, the nation was in a state of disbelief. While the American people had experienced the natural deaths of twelve of their presidents, they had never experienced the assassination of one. Reeling from the events that transpired over a two-day period, the nation questioned how to say farewell in a manner befitting its martyred leader.

Once it had been determined that Lincoln's body would be interred in his hometown of Springfield, Illinois, plans began for numerous funerals and memorial services across the land. The first, by invitation only, was held in the East Room of the White House. The next was held for the public at the US Capitol. From there "The Great Funeral Cortege," as it was called, departed to make several stops along the way.

On April 24, 1865, the cortege arrived in New York City, and Lincoln's body was transported to City Hall to lie in state. Rear Admiral Charles H. Davis of the US Navy stood guard at the head of the coffin, while Brigadier General Edward D. Townsend of the US Army stood at the foot. The two were part of a group selected to accompany Lincoln's body on its final journey.

A New York photographer named Jeremiah Gurney Jr. took photos of the coffin from a balcony above. When Secretary Stanton learned about these photos, he ordered that all plates and prints be sent to him and destroyed out of respect for Lincoln and on behalf of the family's wishes. Yet Stanton could not bear to destroy all of them and retained one print, telling no one about it before his death in 1869.

Some eighteen years later, his son Lewis mailed the print to John Nicolay, who was writing a book with John Hay about Lincoln. Nicolay and Hay had served as Abraham Lincoln's private secretaries. The photo remained in Nicolay's papers, which were donated in 1940 by Helen Nicolay and Alice Hay to the Illinois State Historical Library (now known as the Presidential Library).

The photograph shown here depicts Lincoln in his coffin, flanked by Davis and Townsend. Busts of two of Lincoln's political mentors, Henry Clay and Daniel Webster, are positioned to the left of the coffin. An American flag hangs behind the draped viewing area. The photo is the last image of Abraham Lincoln recorded for posterity. It sadly evokes a stanza from Lincoln's favorite poem, "Mortality." ❧

Soothing Melodies

The Lincolns "Take the Music"

1865 AND 1870

DURING HIS INAUGURAL TRAIN RIDE TO WASHINGTON, AND AT POINTS during his presidency whenever a band serenaded him, Lincoln would often make a short speech and conclude with something like, "Having said this much, I will now take the music." He and Mary loved music, and no wonder. Their musical contemporaries included European composers such as Hector Berlioz, Franz Liszt, and Richard Wagner, and Americans such as George Frederick Root, Daniel Emmett, and Stephen Foster.

Long before Edison had recorded sound, the only way for people to delight in the sound of music, short of attending a live musical performance, was through a music box. One of the prized possessions of the ALPLM's collection is a music box Mary Lincoln acquired sometime shortly after the presidential years. Manufactured in Geneva, Switzerland, the device undoubtedly brought some degree of solace to Lincoln's widow. The music box plays a number of operatic airs including "Maffio Orsini" from *Lucrezia Borgia* and "un foco insolito" ("A Fire Unfelt Before") from *Don Pasquale* by the great Italian composer Gaetano Donizetti. Although Donizetti had died eighteen years prior to Lincoln's assassination, one of his musical compositions was used as a funeral march to memorialize the fallen leader.

It is not known whether Mary ever heard the Donizetti funeral march dedicated to her deceased husband, as she was too distraught to attend any of his funeral services. But she did enjoy the music of Donizetti and others whose compositions were mechanically produced on the music box's brass cylinder. The rectangular casing is made of rosewood, with an inlaid design on its top and front panels, and all parts of the mechanism are still operational. In addition to the Donizetti piece, the box plays operatic airs by Charles Gounod, Friedrich Von Flotow, and Giacomo Meyerbeer, among others.

The music box transports listeners back into Mary Lincoln's parlor, enabling us seven or eight score years later to connect with the former first lady in a very real, intimate way. As Mary might have thought to herself when recalling Abraham, "Now I will take the music." ⌒

A Lincoln coffin fragment and the last artifact directly linked to the president's final moments above ground

Rest in Peace?

Lincoln's Funerary Remnant

1865–1901

88

LINCOLN ONCE WROTE, "IN THIS SAD WORLD OF OURS SORROW COMES to all. . . ." This was most especially true of the sixteenth president himself. His father had lost part or all of the family farm on three successive occasions. Abraham's mother had died of milk sickness when he was just nine years old. During his teenage years, his older sister Sarah died in childbirth, her baby stillborn. His friend Ann Rutledge died at the age of twenty-two, leaving Lincoln bereft. (Historians disagree on whether their relationship was romantic in nature.) His second son, Edward, died before the age of four. His next born, William, died in the White House during Lincoln's first term as president. And of course, President Lincoln lived with the knowledge that his life was under constant threat. Ultimately, he was the first president in the history of the United States to be assassinated.

Even in death, Lincoln's story is one of sorrow. In 1876, inept grave robbers attempted to steal his body from its tomb. Abraham Lincoln could not rest in peace. As the years passed, people continued to question whether Lincoln's body had not in fact been stolen and whether it was still buried in his Oak Ridge Cemetery tomb in Springfield, Illinois. Thus, as the twentieth century dawned, doubts remained, even in the mind of Lincoln's only surviving son, Robert. Determined to allay baseless rumors of another robbery attempt, in 1900 Robert took steps to ensure that his father's remains would never be disturbed again, that he would at last rest in peace. Abraham's and Mary's caskets were moved to another location while the Tomb was rebuilt. On September 26, 1901, Lincoln's casket was ready to be placed ten feet deep under a marble cenotaph. But first the decision was made to open the coffin to quell the rumors. Thus, twenty-three people, mostly workmen, each took a turn peering through the opening at the body which lay beneath, confirming that it was in fact Abraham Lincoln. He had been embalmed so thoroughly and for so long during his twelve national funerals in 1865 that his flesh was still intact. One of the viewers was a thirteen-year-old boy named Fleetwood Lindley. The young Lindley passed away more than six decades later with the distinction of being the last living person to have seen the face of the 16th president. The coffin fragment is the last artifact directly linked to the president's final moments above ground. ⌒

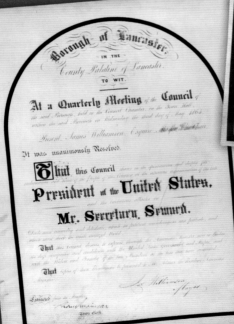

At a Meeting of the Mayor Aldermen and Burgesses of the Borough of Liverpool, in Common Council assembled, held in the Town Hall, within the said Borough on Wednesday, the 3rd day of May 1865.

Present:

Edward Lawrence Esquire, Mayor. &c. &c. &c.

It was unanimously resolved

That this Council desires to record its horror and indignation at the atrocious murder of Abraham Lincoln, President of the United States, and to express its sympathy with the American Nation under their severe loss, as well as to Mrs Lincoln, in the sad bereavement she has sustained.

And it was also resolved

That a Minute of the foregoing Resolution under the Common Seal should be sent to Mrs Lincoln through the British Minister at Washington.

Borough of Lancaster IN THE County Palatine of Lancaster. TO WIT.

At a Quarterly Meeting of the Council of the said Borough, held in the Council Chamber in the Town Hall within the said Borough on Wednesday the third day of May 1865.

Present: James Williamson Esquire Mayor in the Chair.

It was unanimously Resolved

That this Council shares in the universal grief felt throughout this country at the infamous assassination of the late President of the United States,

and the cowardly attack on

Mr. Secretary. Seward.

Lincoln is memorialized on twentieth-century Avon bottles (upper left and lower right), as well as on nineteenth-century proclamations by organizations from across the globe (upper right and lower left).

PART 8
⫷ Icon ⫸

A. Lincoln

89

An Innovative Spirit

Abraham Lincoln—Patent Holder

MARCH 10, 1849

AMERICAN FRONTIER LIFE WAS NOT FOR THE FAINTHEARTED. IT WAS A rough existence, one which required a courageous and entrepreneurial spirit. Growing up on the frontier, Abraham Lincoln understood this. He had an active mind, fertile imagination, and the entrepreneurial and innovative spirit necessary to survive. Faced with a problem, he chose to solve it, which is why it is no surprise that in his fortieth year he developed and received a patent—Number 6,469—for a design he created to buoy boats over riverbed shoals.

The original model for that patent belongs to the Smithsonian Institution. The ALPLM has a recent model made by a skilled hobbyist, and the color copy seen here of the submitted diagram. Lincoln submitted his application and materials on March 10, 1849, and the US Patent Office approved his application on May 22, 1849, for "A. Lincoln's Imp'd [Improved] Manner of Buoying Vessels."

Growing up near rivers as small as Nolin Creek and Little Pigeon Creek, and as broad as the Ohio and Mississippi, and being a one-time riverboat captain on the Sangamon, Lincoln was no stranger to the difficulties of maneuvering vessels up and down stream, avoiding shoals that often caused the water depth to become so shallow that the vessel would run aground. Lincoln's experience gave him the idea to develop a mechanism to lift boats so that they could proceed unimpeded. The approved diagrams for the design exhibits three figures, drawn onto draftsman's paper in a counterclockwise fashion. Written in pencil in the upper left hand corner of the drawing is a price, $2.50, apparently the fee Lincoln paid to submit the application. The prototype model Lincoln helped to make (he hired a professional carver in Springfield for most of it), now at the Smithsonian's National Museum of American History, first went to the US Patent Office. This building still stands today and was the site of Lincoln's Second Inaugural Ball in 1865, chosen by the president himself for, well, you may guess the reason.

Lincoln, the inventor, never moved beyond the design stage with his invention. It is lost to history whether it would have advanced maritime travel. Modern marine engineers say it would have worked on small vessels, but probably not on large ones. While each American president in both his private and public lives accomplishes things uniquely his own, and while all share the titles "president" and "commander-in-chief," only Abraham Lincoln holds the title of "patent holder." ∞

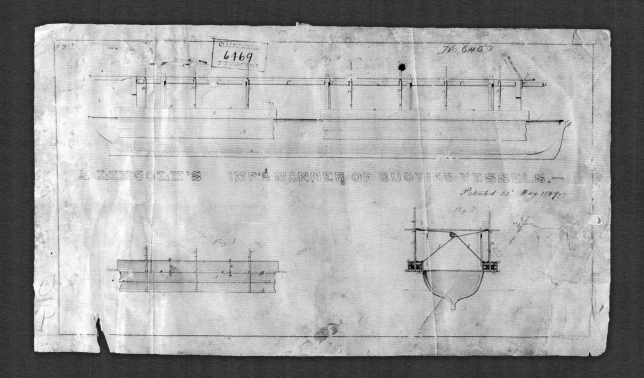

Figure one at the top of the page is a side view of a compartmentalized vessel, with bellows or buoys, fore and aft. Figure two on the right depicts the mechanism of ropes and pulleys for lowering those bellows. Figure three on the left is a magnified view of the vessel's bellows or "expansible buoyant chambers," as Lincoln called them.

90

Quintessentially Lincoln
The Hat That Defined the Man
1856–1860

FEW PEOPLE IN HISTORY HAVE HAD AN ITEM SO INEXTRICABLY LINKED to them as Abraham Lincoln and his stovepipe hat. The one shown here is documented and believed by historians and Lincolniana collectors around the globe to be one of three such hats owned and worn by Abraham Lincoln left in existence. One of the hats is in the collection at Hildene, the family home of Abraham and Mary Lincoln's eldest son, Robert, their only son to live to adulthood. The third hat is in the Smithsonian Institution's National Museum of American History—the hat Lincoln wore to Ford's Theatre on the night of his assassination.

The ALPLM's hat is the oldest of the three and the only beaver-fur stovepipe hat of Lincoln's in existence today. It stands seven and a half inches in height and thirteen and a half inches from front to back, making Lincoln, when he wore it, more than seven

feet tall. It was purchased by Lincoln for about four dollars, a reasonable price for such a hat and about 80 percent less than the cost of a silk one, another popular option at the time. The hat was purchased at a millinery shop owned by Josiah H. Adams on the main square in Springfield, Illinois, sometime in the latter 1850s. The dark brown hat has a narrow silk ribbon at the base of the crown where it meets the brim. A narrow mesh undercoat braid encircles the hat, now visible at the outer edge of the brim. The maker's mark remains distinct and is found on the top of the inside crown of the hat, which is otherwise lined with cotton. The hat's inner leather band frequently held Lincoln's correspondence, legal briefs, and other "hat-sized" notes or documents when he traveled.

Much of the wear and tear came from frequently doffing it to passersby and people Lincoln encountered throughout the day. Hence, the hat featured here is all the more special because of the thumb and finger impressions on it that indicate the gentlemanly proclivities of its owner.

Lincoln gave the hat to William Waller of Jackson County, Illinois, and it was passed down by generations of the Waller family. More so than any other artifact or printed document, the stovepipe hat is quintessentially Lincoln. For people the world over, it is a touching and humanistic symbol of the Great Emancipator and president. ∽

Wellington and Lincoln both ignored the temptation to act or become by force or acclamation a "royal." Yet in artwork and public esteem, they both seemed to reign supreme.

Tall in the Saddle

The Duke of . . . Lincoln?

1861

HERE'S A FIGURINE OF THE DUKE OF WELLINGTON, SITTING ASTRIDE his horse, but with a new head and new raised letters on the base. These mantelpiece decorations from the ceramic capital of Staffordshire, England, which were originally made to pay homage to the deceased duke, were recycled and repurposed for the Lincoln market in 1861. Lincoln never wore an orange cape, nor the duke a beard, yet both sat tall in the saddle.

Lincoln was still largely unknown in 1852 when Wellington died, but his star was clearly on the rise when he was asked to give the main eulogy in Chicago for President Zachary Taylor in 1850, and in Springfield for Henry Clay in 1852. And while president, Lincoln faced down the old French emperor's nephew, the self-styled Napoleon III, who tried to impose a European monarch in Mexico.

There are a number of parallels between Wellington and Lincoln. Napoleon I took a chance by invading Russia in 1812 while the British were distracted by the War of 1812. In 1864 the Frenchman's nephew ignored that old lesson while the real power in North America, Lincoln's federal Union, was tied up against the southern rebellion. Napoleon III sent soldiers, and an Austrian aristocrat, to revive and take the throne in Mexico City. Lincoln did not exactly chase out the French, *a la* Wellington, but the US Navy blunted the French advance, to thwart the imperial ambitions of Napoleon III.

Lincoln also helped create a political echo of Wellington's influence. The duke's death had given Prince Napoleon the symbolic opening he sought to revive the imperial *gloire* of *la France*, styling himself the new emperor. This threat caused major shifts in British political parties, when the Tories and Whigs soon emerged as the Conservatives and Liberals. Lincoln, not sure if he was still a Whig or a new Republican, took up verbal arms and solidified his party's preeminence, just as Wellington had done for his Tories. But where Wellington had strengthened an old party, Lincoln helped give birth to a new one.

The former was a military genius who later took up politics and was considered adept, if not brilliant. The latter was a political genius who was obliged to take a crash course in military command. Wellington and Lincoln both ignored the temptation to act or become by force or acclamation a "royal." Yet in artwork and public esteem, they both seemed to reign supreme. ∞

Out of the Traveling Dark Room

Mathew Brady's Equipment Box

1865

IN 1839, WHEN ABRAHAM LINCOLN WAS THIRTY YEARS OLD, FRENCH-man Louis Daguerre introduced the daguerreotype and with it, the earliest common form of the "photograph" was born. No doubt Lincoln, an inventor and patent holder himself, would have been impressed. The Lincoln era owes much to Daguerre, for without him and his invention, immortal images of the sixteenth president might not exist today.

One of the earliest and greatest American photographers, best known for his photos of both Lincoln and the Civil War, was Mathew Brady, who learned the new art form from renowned American artist and inventor Samuel Morse, who had learned from Daguerre himself. Brady was a quick study, and soon moved beyond studio portraits to become one of the world's earliest photo-journalists. The advent of the Civil War enabled Brady to take his craft to the front and to bring the war home with a realism never before seen except by those who were there to experience it.

Abraham Lincoln, from whom Brady received permission to photograph and document the war, became a frequent subject of the photographer. Innovations after the daguerreotype greatly reduced the developing process, but up until the late 1800s, this process relied on capturing images on glass plates with unwieldy chemicals. To transport and protect the plates, as well as the chemicals and other tools, Brady used a fairly nondescript wooden box onto which he stenciled his name, "M. B. Brady 1865." The box was most probably stored in "the whatizzit wagon," Brady's traveling darkroom, according to the great Lincoln biographer Carl Sandburg. In addition to the box, the ALPLM owns prints of several of Brady's iconic images of Lincoln and the war.

Some of the most famous images by Brady and his staff in the collection shown here are Brady's first photograph of a standing, not-yet-bearded Lincoln, taken in New York in 1860 on the day he delivered his transformational speech at the Cooper Institute, and an 1862 image of a seated, contemplative Lincoln, taken in Washington, DC. Brady and his contemporaries captured in photographs the many dimensions of Lincoln as father, president, and commander-in-chief, but will be most remembered for capturing the compassionate, thoughtful, and contemplative man he was. ∽

93 Thomas Nast and Peace

The End of an Era

APRIL 1865

THE ILLUSTRATION SHOWN HERE SIGNED BY THOMAS NAST IN THE lower left corner doesn't seem to have been published before its appearance in this book.

The supposition is this: Inspired by the pacific sentiments reported in Lee's surrender to Grant at Appomattox on April 9, 1865, and generally having been a pro-Union man, Nast drew this up for *Harper's Weekly* sometime between April 10 and 13 of 1865, expecting to see it in print for the issue dated Saturday, April 22. But Lincoln was killed on April 15 so the news—and art—filling the papers of April 22 and 29 covered that tragedy.

The keen eye of the ALPLM's paper conservator spotted that the whitest parts of this paperboard, the beard on Robert E. Lee and the hair on George Washington, were rendered by Nast's having scraped away the surface of the board. All else here is the deftest of pencil and ink layering and shading to create portraits that were well-known from other engravings or photographs of the era.

Lincoln's pose, interestingly, stems from a photograph taken by Mathew Brady on January 9, 1864. Nast must have liked the tall but not overbearing presence of the leader propping up the middle of the composition and connecting the nation's "head" (George Washington) to its "legs" (the soldier-farmer and his family). Does this scheme place Lincoln as the nation's "heart"?

The Smithsonian Institution's online database SIRIS does not locate Nast's original painting today. We are left, instead, with the brilliant renderings of the era's most remembered cartoonist, a man moved to compositional poetry by the arrival of peace. Or, peace that lasted for five days.

Nast's influence lived on. Grant said in 1868 that he won election to the presidency by "the sword of Sheridan and the pencil of Nast." Rutherford B. Hayes, another Civil War officer, said in 1876 that Nast was "the most powerful, single-handed aide" in his presidential victory.

Nast's politics would change with the times, however. He became a Democrat in 1884, a signal that twenty-four years of rule by the Republicans had run its ideological course. His artwork that year supported Democrat Grover Cleveland to victory, the first Democrat to enter the White House since James Buchanan in 1856. Perhaps that was when the Lincoln era finally ended. ∽

94

"Even the Boldest Held His Breath"

The World Loses a Leader

1865

DURING HIS BRIEF LIFE, ABRAHAM LINCOLN TRAVELED OUT OF THE country only once. Lincoln's presidency primarily focused on domestic issues, with his foreign policy mostly directed at keeping foreign powers, specifically the French and British, sympathetic to and supportive of the Union cause.

News of his death at the hands of an assassin traveled slowly around the world, by combination of telegraph and steamship. It took twelve days to reach London and forty to reach Peking. From that point on, personal and diplomatic condolences began pouring into the nation's capital, as well as to consulates and embassies around the globe. Queen Victoria of the United Kingdom called the tragic event "deplorable," and Prince Kung of China wrote how he was "inexpressibly shocked and startled" by the news. International newspapers led with the news, the *Avenir National* in Paris calling the tragic events "disastrous" and stating that "the great citizen Abraham Lincoln has fallen." "Even the boldest held his breath for a time," wrote Edinburgh's *Caledonian Mercury*. Parliaments and congresses issued proclamations and statements. These were just a few of the ways that officials in distant lands could pay their respects and assuage their grief.

Artists in many countries produced memorial pieces that paid homage to the fallen leader. The ALPLM has five such memorial pieces. The 1865 memorial from France shown here is a silk woven portrait made by Paul Durand in Lyon, France, the French capital for silk weaving. Here Lincoln is framed by laurel and oak leaves symbolizing triumph, strength, and honor. The bald eagle, the American symbol of power and authority along with the Great Seal of the United States, sits beneath the memorialized president.

The memorial print from Spain is also from 1865 and was published by Roca and Brother of Barcelona, a well-known art publisher at the time. The center of the engraving is based on the 1860 photograph by Mathew Brady of a beardless Abraham Lincoln. The print includes an engraving of a scene from Lincoln's funeral in Washington, DC. This print is the only one known to exist about Lincoln from Spain. The silk woven portrait and engraved print are but two examples of the shared grief of the world and Abraham Lincoln's global influence as a man of justice, integrity, and freedom. ∽

Presidente Lincoln.

Mr. Lincoln, who worked with so much earnestness . . . deserved a better fate than the poniard of a coward assassin. —Benito Juarez, president of Mexico

95

Amusements for the Young

The Parlor Monuments Game

1865

Shortly after the death of President Lincoln, various manu-facturers began producing items that not only would keep his memory alive, but also sought to encourage the study of history, including the "illustrious men" who helped advance the nation. One such manufacturer was Oakley & Mason, a New York–based company which produced a game called "Parlor Monuments to the Illustrious Dead."

The three-dimensional puzzle-like game challenges the player to assemble blocks in a proper order and configuration to successfully construct a monument dedicated to an illustrious leader from the past, in this case Abraham Lincoln.

"The Freedman's Monument to Abraham Lincoln," when assembled, reveals a portrait of the slain president, "sacrificed upon the altar of liberty" and paraphrases key sentences from the Emancipation Proclamation.

> I Abraham Lincoln, President of the United States, on this first day of January, in the year of our Lord one thousand eight hundred and sixty-three, do order and declare that all persons held as slaves within the rebellious states are and henceforward shall be free. And I hereby enjoin upon the people so declared to be free to abstain from all violence and labor faithfully for reasonable wages.

Upon constructing "The Children's Monument," the player discovers a touching tribute to the dearly departed sixteenth president:

> Great and immortal chieftain! Though cold and silent, thou art not dead. While standing upon the pinnacle of fame supported by Justice and Mercy, the hand of the assassin was stretched forth to smite thee. That cruel hand thought to consign thee to the tomb, but it bore thee directly to the hearts of the people where thou art still living in all the freshness of thy noble manhood; and where thou wilt forever live. . . . Thine shall be a fame sublime; and the virtues of thy soul Shall, in triumph, onward roll, Until men and nations, free, Blend thy name with LIBERTY. ⤳

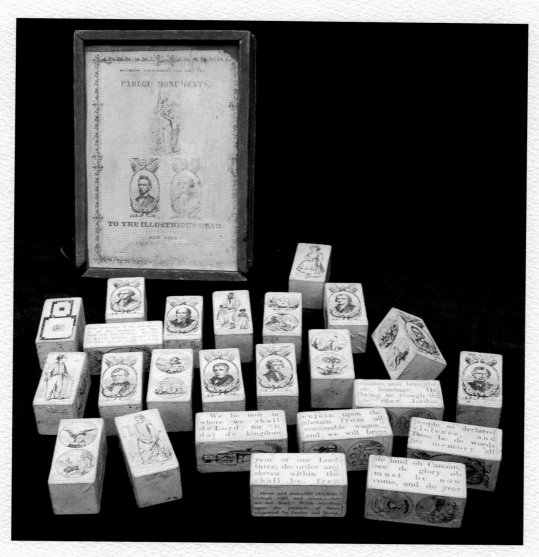

The five monuments that could be built were "The National Monument to George Washington," "The Children's Monument to Abraham Lincoln," "The Freedman's Monument to Abraham Lincoln," "The National Monument to Abraham Lincoln," and "The Presidential Monument." When fully constructed, the shape of any one of the monuments is reminiscent of Lincoln's Tomb. The example in the ALPLM's collection is one of only two known to exist, the other being at Brown University Library in Providence, Rhode Island.

96

A Martyr's Monument

Building the Lincoln Tomb

1869 AND 1885

ABRAHAM LINCOLN'S ASSASSINATION IN 1865 TRANSFIXED THE NATION. It was such a shock and affront that people needed time and ways in which to process what had occurred. One of the many such ways included the contributing to and building of a national monument that would serve as Lincoln's final resting place, in Oak Ridge Cemetery in Springfield, Illinois. Talk of building such a monument began almost immediately upon his death. Its site was chosen by Lincoln's widow, Mary,

A campaign to raise funds for the monument to the "martyr" was mounted by the National Lincoln Monument Association, a group of "memorialists" as they called themselves, organized just twenty-six days after the death of the president. Donations from the public were encouraged and sought. The ALPLM's collection includes a certificate recognizing the fifty-cent donation made by Susan Torrence in 1869, roughly equivalent to twenty dollars in today's money, and was part of the initial funds raised to break ground for the monument. In return for her generosity, Torrence received the certificate signed by James H. Beveridge, who at the time was treasurer of both the state of Illinois, and the Association.

The Lincoln National Monument or tomb was completed in 1874. Although admission to the cemetery was free, it did require a "visitor's ticket." The 1885 ticket bears the names of two officers of the Oak Ridge Cemetery board, Dr. Henry Wohlgemuth, its president, and B. F. Talbott, its secretary. In forming the National Lincoln Monument Association and in soliciting and receiving donations from people across the land like Susan Torrence, the memorialists fulfilled their noble and benevolent mission.

Tens of millions of people have visited the national monument, Lincoln's Tomb, since its opening, to pay their respects to a man of exalted worth. ⚭

But the lofty monument, built by voluntary contributions, will attest the gratitude of his contemporaries for his services, and their appreciation of his virtues, and will excite the emulation of youth, by showing how exalted worth is honored.

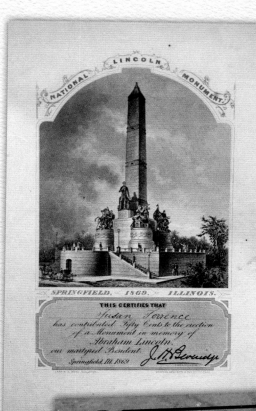

NATIONAL LINCOLN MONUMENT

SPRINGFIELD, 1869, ILLINOIS.

THIS CERTIFIES THAT

Susan Torence
has contributed *Fifty Cents* to the erection
of a Monument in memory of
Abraham Lincoln,
our martyred President.

Springfield, Ill. 1869.

Oak Ridge Cemetery
SPRINGFIELD, ILL.

VISITOR'S TICKET

ADMIT ONE

H. WOHLGEMUTH,
Pres't.

B. F. TALBOTT,
Sec'y.

Lincoln in Your Pocket

Memory in Bronze

1871

COMMEMORATIVE *EXONUMIA*—A LATIN-DERIVED WORD MEANING ALL of the coins, medals, medallets, store tokens, etc., issued in Lincoln's honor—began appearing in droves right after his death. A French-made gold medal in his honor was presented to Mary Lincoln in 1867 and is now in the Smithsonian. The piece shown here dates from 1871, designed by English immigrant William Barber, who sculpted a somewhat surprisingly nude bust of Lincoln working from a photograph that showed him fully clothed. Barber rose to chief engraver at the US Mint in Philadelphia from 1869 to 1879. His son Charles E. Barber followed his father's craft and later designed the "Barber half-dollar" and smaller coins (1892–1916) that depict Lady Liberty looking to the right, in a profile similar to that seen on his father's Lincoln.

The senior Barber did not merely enshrine the deceased president's likeness; on the reverse he added some words from the Emancipation Proclamation. A wreath encloses that nine-line inscription, which includes Lincoln's dates as president and offers as his chief contribution while president that proclamation of January 1, 1863. This medal was part of a series the mint issued at the time, uniting key words with the key figures of American history, at a time when a far greater number of people worked directly with metal and thus, we may assume, had a more direct appreciation for the sculptor's and die-sinker's art. Yet even then government officials in unelected posts took advantage of their station to broadcast their names, for J. Pollock as director of the mint actually had his name and title placed in small raised letters on the back of the coin. It seems that everyone who can connect with Lincoln, does. ∞

Sculpting Lincoln

Daniel Chester French's Maquette

1909

BORN ON APRIL 20, 1850, FAMED AMERICAN SCULPTOR DANIEL CHESter French was a fifteen-year-old when President Lincoln was assassinated. No doubt the shock and horror of the event left an indelible impression on French—an impression he drew upon when planning, modeling, and eventually sculpting the world-renowned figure for the national memorial in Washington, DC.

The year was 1909, the centennial of the birth of Abraham Lincoln, and French was now a fifty-nine-year-old man, working feverishly to create a *maquette*—a preliminary model—of Abraham Lincoln. The bust of Lincoln shown here is made of plaster and coated with a glossy varnish. It is thought to be one of the earliest models for the memorial we know today.

French was chosen for the project by The Lincoln Memorial Commission led by President William Howard Taft. The memorial would occupy the west end of what is known today as The National Mall in Washington, DC. From a seated position in the center of the memorial, Lincoln looks out, gazing toward the Capitol, where he served as a representative in the 30th Congress; took the oath of office as president of the United States; and delivered both his First and Second Inaugural Addresses, the latter of which is inscribed on the memorial's wall opposite the Gettysburg Address.

The planning and construction of the Lincoln Memorial took more than eight years from ground breaking to dedication. When French better understood the scope of the structure designed by American architect Henry Bacon, he decided to triple the size of his sculpture, which was constructed under French's direction by the Piccirilli Brothers. It was dedicated on May 30, 1922, with Robert Lincoln, then age seventy-eight, in attendance along with his wife Mary. French's depiction of Lincoln is thought-provoking, poignant, and awe-inspiring, just as is his early maquette. The model and sculpture capture a contemplative Lincoln whose countenance is not yet ravaged by the effects of war but seems quietly and peacefully touched by the "better angels of our nature." ∽

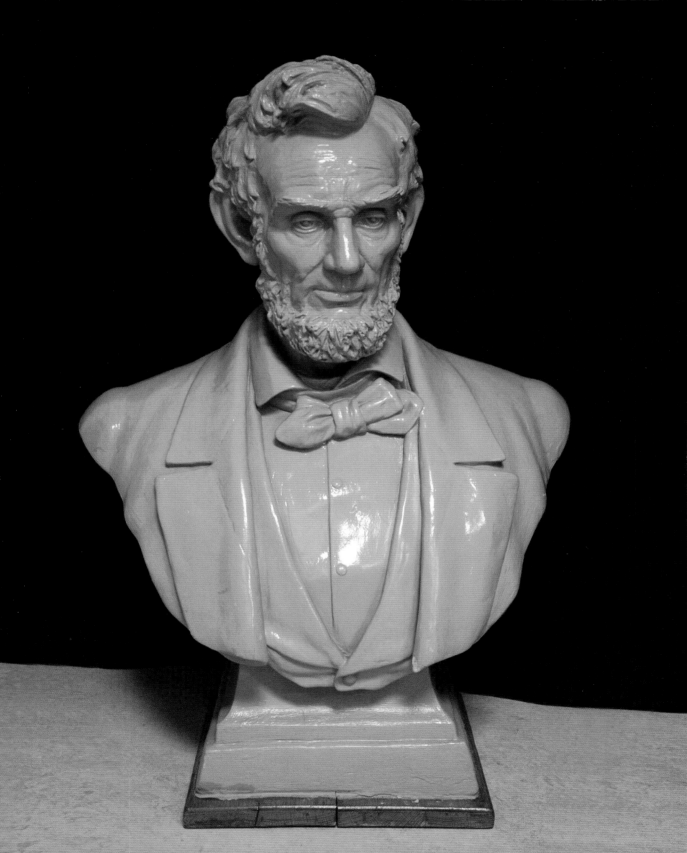

99

Patriotic Artist

Borglum Sculpts Lincoln

1925

ONE OF THE MANY WAYS IN WHICH ABRAHAM LINCOLN HAS BEEN immortalized and cemented into the public consciousness is through the sculpting of the massive monument at Mount Rushmore in Keystone, South Dakota. It was famed American sculptor Gutzon Borglum who in 1927 ventured into the Black Hills and began carving the faces of four great American presidents—George Washington, Thomas Jefferson, Theodore Roosevelt, and Abraham Lincoln—into the façade of a granite mountain. Borglum chose the first three presidents for their respective roles in founding, expanding, and preserving the United States. He selected Abraham Lincoln for reunifying it and bringing "equality" to all.

Borglum, who wore his patriotism on his sleeve, often sculpted and sketched those complexities, as Lincoln was one of Borglum's frequent and favorite subjects. Although Borglum was born two years after Lincoln died, he knew every line, curve, and whisker of the rail-splitter's face, capturing the humanity and countenance of the man in such an extraordinary way that it was difficult to believe the two had never met. Borglum became so adept at sculpting Lincoln that Robert Lincoln, when gazing upon one of the sculptor's pieces responded, "I never expected to see father again."

Standing on an almost six-foot-high square pedestal outside The Treasures Gallery in the Abraham Lincoln Presidential Museum is a plaster head of the sculptor's hero, cast by Borglum or under his direction in 1925. It is the model for a marble sculpture Borglum made that now sits in the Rotunda of the US Capitol in Washington, DC, and was sculpted as Borglum prepared to raise funds for the sculpting of Mount Rushmore. Originally sculpted and cast in 1908, it led to a bronze copy outside Lincoln's Tomb at Oak Ridge Cemetery, where tradition will find visitors rubbing Lincoln's nose for good luck. Other bronzes of the sculpture are located in the states of California and New York. While Borglum gained fame for these sculptures, as well as one in Newark of a seated Lincoln, it was and is his massive granite sculpture at Mount Rushmore for which he is best known. Sadly, Borglum died before the project was completed, but his son, Lincoln Borglum, (named after the sixteenth President), completed the project in 1941. Through his artistic genius, he sculpted, as he said, the "humanity" of Lincoln's "great soul" for our nation and its posterity, giving this larger than life president a larger than life presence for centuries to come. ∞

100

The Better Angels of All Continents

Global Lincoln

2003–2010

GLOBAL TRADE AND IDEAS CERTAINLY GOT A BOOST DURING LINCOLN'S presidency. The movement continues, in part through adulation of Lincoln from all corners of the world. At upper left is a decorative seven-inch woodcut made in 2006 by a Kenyan artist, Ben Z. Nyende, who emigrated to California. At upper right is a book published in Mexico City comparing Abraham Lincoln, Mahatma Gandhi, Reverend Martin Luther King Jr., and Nelson Mandela as four "liberators of the conscience."

At lower left is a book published in the Hindi language in 2010 in New Delhi, called *Ebrahama Linkana* by Dr. Arvind Arora Mukt. At lower right is a four-foot-tall cast sculpture entitled "Before the Day of Decisive Battle." This work, gifted in 2009 to the ALPLM by the sculptor on behalf of the People's Republic of China, opens the doorway into differing interpretations of the sixteenth US president. The sculptor, Xikun Yuan, among the leading artists of his nation, presents Lincoln as a military figure, with field glasses in hand and boot upon an outcropping of rock, ready to use force to keep his nation united. This may be startling to many Americans who think of Lincoln chiefly as an attorney, politician, and writer.

Meanwhile, for the people of India, Lincoln is a man who rose from the depths of dirt-floor Kentucky to the grandeur of white-walled Washington. He is also regarded there as something of a philosopher and teacher, based on a widespread belief that Lincoln once wrote a long list of desiderata to his son's teacher (this was actually composed by someone in the 1970s).

The book by Mexican scholar Juan Maria Alponte, published in 2003, asks the question: If leaders can appeal to the better angels of our nature, would not people everywhere be better off? The doing is never quite as simple as the saying, however, and directing our "nature" toward polyarchic, rather than oligarchic or monarchic rule, has proved extremely difficult in some places. Lincoln inherited a two-party system, protected it, and improved it by insisting upon free elections during wartime. Could his example create a polyarchic system from a base dictatorship? A free society requires many sources of economic and political power, not to mention many books, artworks, and interpretations. It requires a leader like Abraham Lincoln, who can appeal to the better angels of all continents in our increasingly interconnected world. ∽

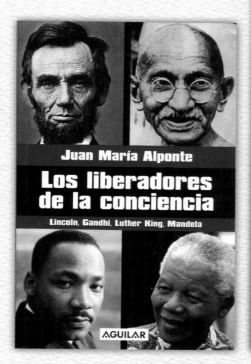

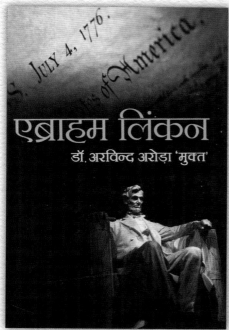

Acknowledgments

On behalf of the Abraham Lincoln Presidential Library Foundation, we gratefully acknowledge Louise Taper not only for contributing the preface for this book, but for her insight into and adeptness at collecting Lincolniana, and, in so doing, helping to preserve our sixteenth president's legacy for the greater global citizenry. We also wish to acknowledge Robert Guinsler at Sterling Lord Literistic, as well as Jim Childs, Holly Rubino, Keith Wallman, Sara Given, Amy Alexander, Jessica Kastner, Ellen Urban, Margaret Milnes, and all those at Lyons Press, whose tireless and committed efforts made *Under Lincoln's Hat* possible. We are privileged to thank our extraordinary colleagues, who, through their hard work and dedication, ensured the successful publication of this book, specifically, Jennifer Blisset, Rene Brethorst, Jennifer Ericson, Phyllis Evans, Ian Hunt, Betsy Londrigan, Sharon Petrilli, Nan Reep, Angela Staron, and Kate Sullivan. Also, we would like to acknowledge the board members and leadership of the Illinois Historic Preservation Agency, Abraham Lincoln Presidential Library and Museum, and Abraham Lincoln Presidential Library Foundation, whose meaningful work on behalf of Abraham Lincoln preserves, protects, and advances his legacy now and for generations to come. Finally, a special word of thanks to Adam Pitluk, without whom the first word never would have been printed. ☙

Gift Acknowledgments

THE ABRAHAM LINCOLN PRESIDENTIAL LIBRARY AND MUSEUM AND the Abraham Lincoln Presidential Library Foundation gratefully acknowledge the following entities and individuals who so generously gifted the following items featured in this book. We apologize for any errors or omissions:

Object 1. Hazel Slate: Gift of Erma Maurice Bowers, Cathy Starr Bowers Dixon, Marcia Lynn Tenney, Richard Douglas Byers, Sue Ellen Sparks

Object 3. Cypher Book Page: Gift of Louise Taper

Object 9. Door Plate: Gift of Jesse Jay Ricks

Object 10. Abraham Lincoln's Letter to Mary Lincoln: Gift of Barrett Fund

Object 11. Mary Lincoln's Letter to Abraham Lincoln: Gift of Barrett Fund

Object 12. Gavel: Gift of West Side Christian Church

Object 12. Candle Snuffer: Gift of J. Allen Henderson

Object 13. Heart-shaped Pendant: Gift of Alice B. Colonna

Object 16. Eddy's Tombstone: Gift of The Edwards Family

Object 19. Whipple's Photo Lincolns at Home in Springfield: Gift of Anson Cooper Goodyear

Object 20. Lock of Hair and Framed Photo: Gift of Patricia and Don Altorfer

Object 21. Company K Photo Album: Gift of Robert Todd Lincoln Beckwith

Object 25. Robert Lincoln's Notes: Gift of Robert Todd Lincoln Beckwith

Object 28. Lincoln's Letter to Welles: Gift of Clinton L. Conkling

Object 32. *The Flush Times*: Gift of Governor Henry Horner

Object 39. First Inaugural Inkwell: Gift of Minnie Smith Johnson

Object 40. The Conkling Letter: Gift of Clinton L. Conkling

Object 41. The Gettysburg Address: Gift of Marshall Field III and the Children of Illinois

Object 42. Edward Everett Notebook: Gift of Marshall Field III and the Children of Illinois

Object 44. "Mortality" Broadside: Gift of Carla Knorowski

Object 45. Heap of Jokes Letter: Gift of David Delano Scherr

Object 53. Life Mask of 1860: Gift of American Academy of Arts & Letters

Object 54. Abraham Lincoln's Briefcase: Gift of Albert and Nicoletta Heyser

Object 60. John Warden's Medal of Honor: Gift of Michael J. Warden

Object 66. Lincoln's Note to Grant: Gift of Barrett Fund

Object 67. Army of the Potomac Axe: Gift of Mrs. A. Clement Wild

Object 72. Emancipation Proclamation Pen: Gift of James and Myra Bradwell

Object 83. *New York Daily News*: Gift of Zale Glauberman

Object 87. Mary Lincoln's Music Box: Gift of Florence Patteson

Object 88. Coffin Fragment: Gift of Louis L. and Leon P. Hopkins

Object 91. The Duke of Wellington Figurine: Gift of Governor Henry Horner

Object 92. Brady Photograph of Abraham Lincoln: Gift of Governor Henry Horner

Object 92. Mathew Brady's Equipment Box: Gift of Michael, Dana, Elise, and Emery Greene

Object 94. Spanish Engraving: Gift of Abraham Lincoln Presidential Library Foundation

Object 98. Daniel Chester French's Maquette: Gift of Benedictine University

Object 100. Statue of Abraham Lincoln: Gift of the sculptor Yuan Xikun

Mary Lincoln's Personal Seal, page 22: Gift of Robert Todd Lincoln Beckwith

Reynolds Jones's *The Circuit Rider*, page 53: Gift of Illinois & Midland Railroad, Inc., A Genesee & Wyoming Company

Mary Edwards Brown Photo, page 61: Gift of Mary Edwards Brown

Lincoln's Wax Seal on Paper, page 74: Gift of Harry Pratt

Ceramic Ink Bottle, page 74: Gift of Renee M. Housel

Gold Pen Set, page 75: Gift of Margaret Porter Davis

Walking Stick, page 94: Gift of Louis G. and Adrienne Lower

Campaign Lantern, page 96: Gift of Lois Jazo Family in Memory of A. Larry Jazo

Lincoln at Richmond Engraving, page 112: Gift of Betty Hickey

Lincoln's Wax Seal, page 113: Gift of Harry Pratt

Emancipation Engraving, page 147: Gift of Betty Hickey

White Avon Bottle, page 190: Gift of Wayne R. Athurton

Abraham Lincoln Portrait, page 191, Gift of the LeRoy Neiman Foundation

Index